Every Day It Got Better

Enrico Togna

VANTAGE PRESS
New York

Published by Vantage Press, Inc.
516 West 34th Street, New York, New York 10001

Manufactured in the United States of America
ISBN: 0-533-14019-6

Library of Congress Catalog Card No.: 01-130708

0 9 8 7 6 5 4 3 2 1

To my wife, Bette, our children, and grandchildren

Contents

Part I: Early Years

Part II: 1945–50, My Navy Years

Part III: I Finally Made It—Tough All the Way

Part I

Early Years

1
It All Started This Way

My father came to the United States as a member of a crew on a ship after the First World War after serving a few years in the Italian army. He lost a brother in the army. He was a motorcycle soldier and was decapitated while on duty by a wire strung across the road.

My father, Tony, jumped ship in either Quebec or Montreal, Canada. He had a sister in Hamilton, Ontario. To make a living while living in Canada, Tony went to work with smugglers. They smuggled Canadian whiskey across the St. Lawrence River to New York State. They had to work the nights that there was no moon. They would load the rowboat with all the whiskey it would hold and row across the river to New York State. One night while still in the river they were fired at by U.S. marshals. Tony said they turned the rowboat over and dumped all the whiskey in the river so they wouldn't be caught with it and let the boat drift away as a decoy. The river current was strong, and they drifted for a while before they made it to shore. As they were in an unfamiliar place and did not speak English, it was a couple of days before they realized they had come ashore on the New York State side of the river. The river was over a mile wide. Tony did not want to chance swimming it in the daytime for fear of being caught, and forget it at night. Doing odd jobs and washing dishes in diners, he worked his way to New York City.

They found Little Italy and with help from newfound friends learned the ropes. Tony went to construction sites and got in a line with twenty to thirty men in it every day. They called this shaping up. While in line day after day, Tony learned to speak English. You waited for someone on the job to get hurt or someone to not come to work; the first one in line got hired. As long as you did not get hurt and showed up every day, you had a job. It was a couple of weeks before Tony got hired. Tony lived like that, bouncing around from place to place, for a year or so.

Then one spring Tony landed a job with a road-building contractor, building a section of concrete highway from New York City to Albany, New York, in the town of Mahopac. The men who were working on the road would rent rooms from families along the way. Some families served food, too. Sometimes the crew would be in an area for a long time. Because of the terrain, the Lake Mahopac section was one of those areas. Road building was difficult. Tony and a few of the other men in the crew got rooms and board with an Italian family that took in boarders in a town not too far away from the work, in Brewster, New York. Tony became friendly with the Spiotti family, who ran the boardinghouse. Mr. Spiotti was a foreman of a railroad crew of about ten men who made sure the railroad tracks that went to New York City were in good repair. Mr. Spiotti was to keep the railroad tracks from Millwood to Hopewell Junction, about fifty miles, in working order at all times, twenty-four hours a day. Mrs. Spiotti took care of the house, garden, chickens, pigs, her children, and the boarders with her oldest daughter, Arcangela. The other children who could help with the chores worked, too.

After the first snowfall, construction work outside usually stopped until March. Most of the men went home to friends or relatives for the winter. Mr. Spiotti needed extra men in the winter to keep the tracks opened so the trains could take people to work in New York City. He asked Tony if he wanted to work clearing snow. Tony worked for Mr. Spiotti all winter on the railroad tracks. There was a turntable in Mahopac where they had to turn the train engines around several times a day. They had a switching station there, too. Mr. Spiotti was always looking for good help. Tony worked on the railroad tracks for a year or so. Tony ended up marrying Arcangela. She was called Maggie. They were married July 31, 1927.

I don't know when my father, Tony, and my mother, Maggie, ended up in Avon, Connecticut, working on a farm for a wealthy man, Mr. Patemo. What Mr. Patemo did for a living I don't think Tony ever knew. He was a good man and very generous, I remember my father saying. Every time Mr. Patemo came up to the farm from New York City, he would give Tony a handful of cigars; they were worth one dollar apiece at that time. All that Tony knew was that Mr. Patemo had invested heavily in the stock market.

In 1929 the stock market crashed, and a few months later Mr. Patemo jumped out of a nineteenth-floor office in New York City. The family made some kind of arrangement with Tony about the farm. They wanted the main house as a retreat whenever they wanted to visit the farm. That was no problem in those days, leaving a house unoccupied for weeks; it did not matter. There was no water in the house, and heat, when needed, was provided by a fireplace or wood stove. The main house was wired for electricity; they had a generator to produce DC electric power from a water wheel that was rigged up by a stream near the house. It worked when there was enough water to go over a little man-made dam to make the water wheel turn. In the summer months, the stream was usually dry from lack of rain.

Tony worked the farm a couple of years. Maggie had two children when they lived on the farm, a girl, Lina, born in May of 1930, and a boy, Michael, born in January of 1932. I don't remember when Lina or Mike arrived; they were just there.

As I got older a situation or a happening or a circumstance would leave me inquisitive. The story to this point is written from stories I heard at different times. This is how I pieced the story together. But, I do remember things that happened on the farm as early as the summer of 1932, especially if they were out of the daily routine. I was three and a half years old then.

The first story to come to mind happened in 1932. We had a German shepherd that was used to herd the cows or the sheep whenever Tony sent the dog out to fetch them. Tony was mowing hay with a team of horses when the shepherd chased a rabbit in front of the cutting bar on the mowing machine, spooking the horses. Tony could not stop the team in time, and cut off a hind foot on the shepherd. The dog's leg healed really well in a few weeks. He was running around doing his work again. He was not as fast as he used to be. Tony and I, with the shepherd, were moving the sheep from across the road through the yard heading for another pleasure for the sheep to graze. The dog would tease the ram, snipping and barking loudly at him. This day the ram did not scare and chased the shepherd. The dog was not as agile as he used to be. He ran back to his doghouse for safety; the ram followed the dog right into the doghouse and butted the dog through the back of the doghouse. I had a stick and I chased the ram off the dog. I didn't think anything about the ram coming after me. I remember all the animals would move away from me as long as I had a stick in my hands.

The water wheel that made electricity for the main house was not turning now. I used to play in it. The wheel was about seven feet in diameter, had an axle about twelve feet long that lay on two concrete pillars that were surrounded by a pool of water about three to four feet deep and about twelve to fifteen feet across. I was three and one half years old. I used to shimmy out on the axle to the wheel and play in the wheel. The wheel had spokes and cross braces throughout. I would swing on them like a monkey. Whenever it rained really hard and long, there would be enough water to turn the wheel. I enjoyed playing in the water wheel, when it was turning more than when it was still.

One day my mother was looking for me and my father to come in for lunch, my father was fixing a piece of machinery that broke, and whenever we were near the barn I would go and play in the water wheel. The wheel was turning, I was inside, I saw Mom, and I hollered to my mother, "Look at me!" or something on that order. My mother went nuts. She couldn't come to the wheel; the water around it was too deep. She found my father and told him to get me before I got hurt. My father was laughing and told her that I played in it all the time: "When I can't find him I know where he is."

In the fall of 1932 my uncles would come to the farm from Brewster, New York, to hunt often. They were my mother's brothers. They would hunt small game as well as deer. They would leave some of their kill with my mother.

Around Thanksgiving time my father would butcher a pig and a steer; that was always a big event. My uncles and Grandpa Spiotti would come to the farm on that day. When they went home that evening they went home with half of the kill.

Another event that sticks in my mind: I was about four years old. I was with my father all the time. He was milking the cows one evening. He had only one lantern left that worked; the others were broken, needing either a wick or a new glass. I was always running and jumping even then. If I wasn't sleeping, I was always doing something. My father had to carry the lantern with him to do his chores, including milking. While milking he put the lantern down. I would come running down the aisle and jump over the lantern. I would do this over and over. My father kept telling me each time to stop, not to do that. "You will get hurt; you will break the lantern; you might start a fire." Well, you can guess it. I knocked the lantern over and broke it, spilling oil all over, and it caught on fire. My father had to use the milk he had in the pail to put the fire out—the first time and only time I got a spanking. I was hurt more from the fact that my father hit me than from the pain of the spanking. He worked the rest of the night in the dark, and I went to the feed room and went to sleep. Tony had to work in the dark in the morning, too.

Later that day Tony had to go to town. It was a project; he had to hitch the team of horses to the sleigh because there was snow on the roads. Tony got enough glass and wicks to fix all the broken lights. That night the barn was lit all over.

While Tony and Maggie were on the farm in Avon, Connecticut, my grandfather, Mr. Spiotti, bought a piece of property in Lake Mahopac, about 200 feet and 600 deep from the road. The railroad tracks bordered the back of the property. It was less than a half-mile to the turntables and train yard where Grandpa worked out of. They moved in to a new duplex in the fall of 1931. They had chickens, pigs, and a vegetable garden over one acre.

2

Everything Was a Mystery

During the rest of the winter in 1931 and 1932, except when Mike was born, Aunt Edith came to live with us for a while. Everything was normal. I would go to Grandma and Grandpa's once in a while for a few days at a time during the year. I don't know what actually happened early in 1933. I do remember that me and my sister, Lina, and brother, Mike, were taken to different homes to live for a few months in the city of Cold Springs in New York State. I was told that my mother and father had taken ill and were in the hospital.

I lived with a middle-aged couple who had a grown son who was an up-and-coming boxer. He was next in line to fight the champion, in what weight class I don't know. I don't remember their name, either. I lived with them like I was their younger son. I had the run of the house. This guy was in his early twenties. He would get up early in the morning while it was still dark and run. He would be back when the rest of us got up and ready to eat breakfast. This man could eat. His mother just kept on giving him more and more. During the day he would run; sometimes I would run with him. When I got tired he put me on his back and ran for a while like that. We would go out on the Hudson River, and he would row for hours up and down the Hudson River. One day while rowing into the dock after rowing all afternoon, we were in about three and a half to four feet of water. The water was clear. We could see the bottom with no trouble. An eel was coiled up on the bottom of the river enjoying the sun. The boxer stuck the oar into the middle of the coil and flipped the eel into the rowboat, which was about twelve feet long. The eel was three inches in diameter and about seven feet long. It kept crawling out of the boat, and the boxer was flipping the eel back in the boat. I was trying to stay clear of the eel and the boxer's oar. Every time he flipped the eel into the back of the boat, I went to the front, and vice versa. This went on for a long time. The boxer seemed to be enjoying it. I was half scared to death. Finally, the eel stopped. I don't know if he hit it to kill it or it drowned from all the tossing around.

My sister, Lina, lived a half-block away on the corner of the same street I lived on. Lina lived right on the waterfront of the Hudson River. These people had a restaurant and bar. I used to run down to see her every third day or so. Our brother, Mike, lived across the railroad tracks by the hospital. One day Lina and I decided to go and see Mike. Or I decided Lina would go with me to see Mike is more like it. Whenever I would go to see Lina about noontime the people Lina lived with would give me something to eat. This day when asked what I wanted, I said, "I don't have time. Lina and I have something to do." We walked up the street over the railroad tracks and in the general direction of where I was told the hospital was. We walked for blocks, turning every couple of blocks left or right, whichever way I thought was the way to the hospital. Well! We do find the hospital; now which house does Mike live in? We walked around the hospital hoping to see Mike outside of one of the houses. By then it was late in the afternoon and the people who were taking care of Lina were wondering what happened to us. They called the police. Living right next to the Hudson River, they were thinking the worst. We were not at the house I lived at, nowhere on the streets or in the backyards in the area.

I decided to go into the hospital to ask if they ever had a little boy named Mike Togna come in sick in the last few days. (Mike was always sick.) Then I asked if my mother, Maggie Togna, was in this hospital. The lady at the office said to wait here and she would check. In a little while two policemen came into the office. I can still see their faces, with big smiles, happy to see us. They each scooped us up in their arms and thanked the lady and took us home.

I was grounded. I couldn't even go out in the backyard by myself, and it was fenced in. All the yards were fenced in. A week or so went by and I was being trusted a little more each day. I drove a hard bargain. I begged every day to go out. I finally got my freedom back, and I was back to the way it was. A few more days go by, and the two women who took care of Lina and me went for a walk with us. After a while I realized we are going toward the hospital. I turned and asked them, "Are we going to see Mike?" and they said yes. Lina and I were overjoyed, jumping all over the place. The women kept telling us to calm down. Mike did live near the hospital, two blocks away on the farthest side of the hospital. Every couple of weeks these two women would take Lina and me to see Mike. Around the middle of October 1933, Lina, Mike, and I finally met our mother at Grandma's house in Lake Mahopac. Maggie had a black patch over her left eye and was holding a baby in her arms. Maggie had another son on the twenty-fourth of June 1933. His name is Tony, Jr., after his father. My father was nowhere to be found.

When Lina, Mike and I asked where Tony was, the answer was, "He is working and can't come home." We were at Grandma's for about a week. Then my mother, Lina, Mike, and I moved into a little house about a mile from Grandma's. The baby, Tony, Jr., stayed with Grandma. The winter of 1933 and 1934 was very cold and snowy. The snow on the ground was twenty inches deep, and another storm started, wind blowing and snowing coming down all night. The doors and windows were so drafty the snow blew into the house. My mother poked newspaper in the cracks around the door and windows in the kitchen and closed off the rest of the house. We only had a two-burner kerosene stove for heat. We huddled around the kerosene stove all night. My mother was awake all night trying to stop the snow from coming in the room. I was up to try to help her.

The next morning at daybreak the sun was out, the storm was over, but it was very cold. As my mother was making oatmeal, my Uncle John comes bursting through the door, bringing snow, knocking all the paper out of the door that Mom and I spent all night poking in the doorjamb, and the cold air came in. My mother starts hollering at John, her brother, calling him all kinds of names except John. My Uncle John was only five or six years older than I was. My mother starts hitting him with the broom. John is trying to defend himself. Maggie says, "Can't you knock before you come in?"

There was no key for the door. By the time we got most of the snow outside and the door closed, Maggie had put the oatmeal that she was cooking in the sink. Guess what? It was frozen. Maggie started to hit her brother John again with the broom. I grabbed the broom to stop her. Maggie sat down on the floor and started to cry. Uncle John put the oatmeal back on the stove, and he helped to put the paper back in the doorjamb. We sealed everything up again against the cold. Uncle John stayed a few more hours. Lina, Mike, and I played with him for a while, and John got Maggie to laugh. Uncle John left by going out a window; the snow was that deep, and it was easier to seal up again. The next day about noontime there was a knock on the door. Some men in the area were going around digging people out of their homes. Later that day I went to Grandma's and got some supplies. The snow was over my head. We survived the winter.

That spring we moved to another house in Mahopac Falls. It was a six-family house, and we had rooms on the third floor, on the left side of the house. There were four rooms and a bath. Kids were all over the place. This place was about three miles from Grandma's. For the first time Tony, Jr., came to live with us. We did not see Grandma or Grandpa the whole summer. The only one we saw was Uncle John, now and then. I got up early every day, ate something for breakfast, and was gone all day until suppertime. I would play in the fields, woods, or ponds, with whoever was out there, too! If no one was around I would play by myself. One day I came upon a pond that had a lot of bullfrogs in it. I played all day in the water with the frogs. When I went home for supper I brought a big bullfrog home with me. My mother asked where I was. I told her I was playing with a whole bunch of frogs like this one. Maggie took the frog that I had become friends with on the way home to the sink and hit it over the head and we had it for supper with whatever else Maggie made for us to eat. As I went out to play after breakfast the next day Maggie said to me, "See if you can catch a few more frogs for supper tonight." I played outside all day. When I was ready to go home I had trouble trying to bring two frogs home. They kept getting away from me. In order to get them home I had to hit them over the head. Now I could carry four frogs home. I did this on and off all summer. In early summer I would find strawberries in the fields. I would eat all I wanted, then pick a quart-sized mayonnaise jar full and bring them home for everyone else to eat. Maggie would send me out for more.

Uncle John would come by once in a while to see how things were. We would go fishing along the shore of Lake Mahopac. John was a good fisherman; we all caught a lot of fish. He would give us half of his fish and take the rest to his home for Grandma.

The first of September 1934, all of us moved in with Grandma at Lake Mahopac. My uncles, four of them, Nick, Joe, Eugene, and John, were in one room. The bedrooms were big; all the rooms in the house were big. My mother, Lina, Mike, the baby, Tony, Jr., and I were in another bedroom. One aunt, Edith, was in a tiny room that used to be the linen closet. The bed just fit in the room with a little cabinet.

I started school, first grade. My Uncle John took me to school. We lived about two and one-half miles from the school. It was halfway around the lake. We walked to school. Everyone in school walked to school.

When I started school I did not know many English words, I could not read the reader, and I did not know many more words in Italian. Grandma could only speak Italian. I knew only enough Italian to get by. The whole neighborhood spoke nothing but Italian. I learned fast. By the first of November I was reading. The kids finally stopped teasing me about my reading. A couple of weeks before Thanksgiving I was told we were going to see my father on Thanksgiving weekend. I would ask, "Where is he? What is he doing?" The answer was always the same; it didn't matter who I asked: "You will have to wait and see."

That Saturday after Thanksgiving, Grandpa and Grandma, Maggie, the baby, Tony, Jr., and I got into Grandpa's car and drove about one hour to Ossining, New York, right on the Hudson River. In Ossining there is a New York State prison. My father was in jail. I didn't know this then. All I knew was Tony had to stay there with the other men and work until the job was done. I asked what kind of job it was that it took all those men to do the work; no one knew. We would go see Tony every three or four weeks.

This winter was as bad as last winter with another three-day snowstorm, a lot of snow, and very cold temperatures (winter 1934–35). Grandpa was working around-the-clock keeping the railroad tracks clear of snow. He had all his sons working with his crew to help with the snow. This awful storm started a few days before Christmas; the storm was in its second day. All the men were working around-the-clock; they would get a little sleep at the railroad yard. They slept with their clothes on to be ready to help the others who were working, if need be. My grandmother liked me a lot; she always showed a lot of affection. At the height of the storm my Uncle John came in out of the storm, cold and hungry, around midnight. Grandma fed John and made a lot of tuna fish sandwiches with homemade bread. John said, "The men want coffee." Grandma made coffee and filled a couple of one-gallon jugs.

Over an hour later, Uncle John did not come back. The wind was still blowing hard, and it was still snowing, too. All the adults were up, ready for whatever needed to be done. With all the noise and commotion going on, I

16

was wide awake, too. Grandma asked me if I knew where the turntable for the train engines was. I said I knew. Grandma said to me, "Do you think you can bring the men some coffee?" I said yes. Now, this briefing with Grandma, Aunt Edith and my mother helped to clarify what I was to do. Aunt Edith and Maggie dressed me up in winter clothes. Grandma gave me two one-gallon jugs. I went out the cellar door in the back of the house, which is ground level, and the railroad tracks were straight back about six hundred feet. When I got to the railroad tracks I was to turn right and follow the tracks to the yard, which I did with a lot of difficulty. I basically dragged the jugs through the snow until I got to the railroad tracks. The snow on the tracks was not as deep. About a quarter-mile to go. When I got to the turntable area my grandfather could not believe what he saw as I came out of the darkness into the light. The men gave a big "hoot-la" as I came closer. The men enjoyed the coffee even though it was barely warm. Grandpa said, "Can you find your way home?"

I said, "Yes!"

"Tell Grandma we need more sandwiches."

I made three more trips by five o'clock in the morning. When I came back from the last trip I lay down to rest before I went out again. I fell asleep and the women didn't have the heart to wake me up (or is it they had heart?). My Aunt Edith took the food out to the men. When Edith came back I woke up and wanted to know what was going on. Edith said I came into the kitchen and went over to the corner in the kitchen and just lay down and went to sleep. Things were back to normal in a day or so.

That weekend we went to see Tony in Sing Sing Prison. During the storm the women talked freely about

Tony being in prison and about how much longer he would be there. I don't know if they knew I was paying attention or not. I knew Tony was in jail for being bad. I could not find out what bad thing my father did.

I played by myself most of the time. There was no one for me to play with. This was early in the spring of 1935. One day after lunch I went out to play in the driveway of the tenants' side of the duplex where we lived, which Grandma owned. The driveway sloped from the road downward to the back of the house. The cellar door was grade-level in back of the house. There were stones in the driveway, and I would pick up a stone and throw it at a target stone in the stone wall that made the foundation of the house. I was playing a game running up and down the driveway throwing stones at a big stone cemented in the foundation wall. Well, I got careless and threw a stone too high. It bounced off of the top of the wall through a window in the tenants' living room and the stone hit a family heirloom that was handed down one generation after another for over two hundred years. It broke into several pieces. As my grandmother and this old lady were screaming at each other in Italian, I went into the house to see what all the fuss was about. Whatever the heirloom was, it was in small pieces now. When this old lady saw me in her living room she came at me screaming. Grandma got between us. From what I found out later the words she used on me (to coin a phrase) would make "the devil cover his ears." That was the first time I was ever in that side of the house. Grandma told me to go. I went to Grandma's side of the house. These two women argued for a long time. When Grandma came in she looked terrible. She was hunched over and looked beat. Grandma and Maggie got into hollering at each other in Italian. That was the first time I ever saw them

18

argue with each other. Aunt Edith was always arguing with Grandma. After a while Maggie grabbed me by the arm and dragged me upstairs to our bedroom.

Maggie started to hit me, first slapping me and yelling at me, asking me why I was always a bad boy. Every time I denied that I was bad I got slapped or punched. I went from wall to wall. At one point I was able to crawl under the bed. I was crying all the time. Maggie was saying to stop crying. She would rant and rave for a few minutes, then pull me out from under the bed. I could not understand what Maggie was saying to me. Maggie started to hit me again. I was scared. I don't know if she was ever going to stop. I started to hit Maggie. Every time Maggie hit me I hit her back. This didn't work so well; it only made her madder. After a few minutes of our counterpunching each other, Grandma came in our room and made Maggie stop. I cried and whimpered all night and the next day. I think I was crying more for the fact that my mother had to beat me rather than from the aches and pains. I felt all over. I had bumps, cuts, and black-and-blue marks everywhere.

Maggie never hit us children, and Maggie never hit me again. (That episode was enough for a lifetime.) The result of the argument Grandma and Maggie had prior to my beating was that Grandma said we had to leave and, of course, Maggie went nuts.

Well, as luck would have it, if you want to call it luck, there was a house for rent across the railroad tracks and Route #6, a state highway. The house was about fifteen hundred feet from Grandma's, more or less. To get to Grandma's from the new place we moved into, we went about one hundred feet across Route #6, about five hundred feet across an open lot to the railroad tracks, one hundred feet across three sets of tracks to the edge of

Grandma's property, then six hundred feet to her house. The five of us moved into the house, Maggie, Lina, Mike, Tony, Jr., and me. From then on Grandma never had much to say to me. I felt real bad, for she was the only one in the whole family who had shown any affection. My uncles always teased me, only more so now. Uncle John was still nice to me. He had to come to the house and do the heavy chores that I could not do.

Guess how I learned to swim? Self-taught! We lived a quarter of a mile from Lake Mahopac. I'd be on the dock and my uncles Nick and Eugene would catch me and throw me into the lake. I nearly drowned. Uncle John came to my rescue. John said, "I'll show you how to do the doggy paddle. They will catch you off guard again and they will keep throwing you off the end of the dock until you are enjoying it." After a couple more times off the end of the dock I was not scared anymore. They finally quit throwing me off the end of the dock.

3

Started to Live As a Family Again

Sometime in the spring of 1935 Tony got out of jail. He went to work for a farmer in a town called Mondia. We moved into a four-room flat on the third floor of a twelve-family tenement house in the town of New Windsor. I started school in the second grade in the town of Vails Gate. We all walked to school; it was almost three miles.

Tony had to walk almost five miles to work. Tony got up at three o'clock in the morning, had a cup of coffee and some cookies, and went to work at the farm. We would not see him again until about 8:30 P.M. The farmer Tony worked for would feed him lunch.

On Sunday mornings I would get up early and go with Tony to work. Sunday morning after milking and a few chores, the work done, we went home until three-thirty Sunday afternoon and Tony would have to go to work again to milk the cows. Sometimes I would go with him.

In January, right after the New Year of 1936, Tony rented a house in Mondia, about a half-mile from the farm he worked on. That meant he got up at 4:00 A.M. instead of 3:00 A.M. and he got home earlier at night, around 7:30 P.M. I had to change schools in the last half of the second grade, in 1936. I went to a school in Cornwall. The school was four miles away, but I only had to walk a half-mile to get a bus to school. There was a bully in the second grade who kept picking on me. He didn't want anyone playing with me. No one did. It didn't bother me. I was used to being alone. I did not need anyone to play with. This frustrated him, and he wanted to know why I didn't care. I told him I didn't like people. Well, this kid tried his damnedest to bribe me to want to belong and play with the other kids. My brother and sister were not old enough for school yet.

My mother gave birth to a baby girl sometime in May 1936. The baby's name was Helen. I remember changing the baby and feeding her now and then. After school was out Maggie would take all of us around quitting time to the farm where Tony worked a couple of times a week.

Not far from the farm there was a bridge on Route #9 over Mondia Creek. It was almost dried up from lack of rain, just a little water running through it. We were playing on the bridge. I was throwing stones in the water, watching them splash. All of a sudden Maggie let out a scream. The baby had fallen out of her arms and into the marshy and weedy part of the creek. I ran to the end of the bridge that was close to the driveway to the farm. I got to the baby and everything was fine. The baby was still all bundled up in her blanket but wet and muddy. By the time I got the baby to the driveway, Tony, the farmer, and a few more people were there. The farmer's wife took the baby and my mother to the house. We kids stayed outside the house and barn until Tony was done with his work and we all went home for supper.

I thought things were all right. The next day Maggie had a nervous breakdown and a doctor came to the house. I don't know what happened to Maggie. She wanted to sleep all the time. Maggie seemed to be lazy and was always tired. My mother was suffering from what they called postpartum depression. Evidently after every child

Maggie would go into a postpartum depression, and I remember Aunt Edith would come and stay with us for a while at different times. I did not know this at the time. I was told Maggie was sick; that's all. Tony and the doctor committed Maggie to a hospital in Middletown, New York. In a couple of days Grandma and Grandpa were at the house in Mondia. Grandma and Tony argued all day.

Tony had to go to work; it was time to milk the cows. Grandma took Lina, Mike, and Tony, Jr., with their clothes, and she and Grandpa left. I was left home with the baby, Helen. I had to feed the baby and change her when needed. I was about seven and a half years old at that time. My father came home around 7:00 P.M. and fixed something for us to eat. He bathed Helen and made up some food and gave me instructions for the next day. We had rabbits and chickens that I had to feed and water. We had electric lights but still had an icebox and wood-burning stove. I had to go for water out into a pasture where there was a spring that a half-dozen people used for water. I used to carry two three-gallon pails at a time when I went for water. When the family was all together, I used to make four, maybe five trips a day. The spring was about five hundred feet from the house. I went for the water every day, rain or shine, hot or cold. I stayed home and took care of Helen about ten days. Then someone came over one night and Tony gave this woman Helen and some clothes.

Now I had a different job to do. Every evening when Tony and the farmer started to milk the cows, with the first cow they milked I was given a two-quart milk pail and delivered it to the people who had Helen. They lived about five miles from the farm. After a couple of days of going on the road, coming back to the farm I would take a shortcut through the fields and woods and I found Mondia Creek. I followed the creek to where Helen had fallen into it, next to the farm's driveway. I used to play in the creek. I would catch a frog now and then; the big ones I would kill and bring home for supper. I would catch a fish with my bare hands sometimes. I would swim in the deep holes in the creek and kill snakes when I saw one.

The rest of the summer it was just me and my father. I would follow him everywhere. They worked the farm with horses and mules. Sometimes Tony would spend the whole day in the field, plowing or cultivating or mowing. He would send me to the farmer's house for sandwiches and water.

The farmer was neglecting his farm and family. He would go out at night to a tavern, and sometimes Tony and I would be walking to work at 4:30 A.M. and we would be coming to the bridge by his driveway and see a car going to the house. Tony would mumble over his breath, "I'm not getting any help milking this morning." I would help carry the milk pails to the milk house and wash the cows' utters. There were a couple of gentle cows that I could milk. It wasn't long before the farmer had lost his farm and wife. They had a sale and sold everything. I didn't know what was going on, and the answer I would get was, "You are too young to understand."

A day or two after the sale a truck came to the house and we loaded everything in the house on the truck. We moved to another farm that Tony went to work for in Montgomery. The farm that was then, in 1936, is now a piece of Stewart Air Force Base. They took all 300 acres of the farm. The house was a two-family one. The other worker on the farm lived in the other side of the house with his wife. The woman was very nice.

4

Everything Went Downhill

I always got picked on in school and usually got whipped. I had no one on my side. I was always alone. The other boys had friends on their side. This one time, this boy was on top of me wrestling and his younger brother was trying to drop a large stone on my head. Within the minute, I pushed the kid off and beat them both so they were hurting. This changed my thinking. I must hit back sooner. This was an ongoing thing. Our family moved at least twice a year, so I went to two different schools for each grade until the fifth grade. I always had to fight the bully in the class. There was always a smart kid, a dumb kid, a bully, a coward, a clown, a squealer, and a lookout in each class, the rest of the kids were mediocre. I was mediocre—other than my clothes. I wore blue jeans and workshoes to school and was badly in need of a hair cut. "I was country when country wasn't cool." So, I stood out among the rest of the kids. I was a shy and foolish kid. I was always put to the test by the bully of the class. I was harassed, teased, taunted or mocked. I did not defend myself verbally. After a few days, the bully became real sure of himself and would strike me. I was not one to start a fight, I was a counterpuncher, but all the anger and hate I was harboring would come out with such force that when I hit back, I either knocked him to the ground or hurt him real bad. The fight would usually end with one punch from me.

For awhile everyone would avoid me, as time went by, though, one by one I was accepted by everyone. Every time I started a new school, I went through this routine. I never thought to kill anyone to get even. Guns were always used in my family. They were used as a tool for a certain job, just as a shovel, pitch fork, baseball bat or whatever. The teaching in those days was to be fair minded even in an unfair situation.

The week before school was to start, Grandpa showed up with Lina and Mike with their clothes. Grandma kept Tony, Jr., with her. Grandpa and Tony talked all afternoon until it was time to milk the cows. I was showing Lina and Mike everything I had discovered while I was there by myself. The lady next door took us to school to register for classes in the town of Montgomery. I started third grade, Lina started first grade, and Mike was to start kindergarten. We walked about a thousand feet from the house to the road and caught a bus to a school that was about five miles away.

Everything was going along just fine. I was enjoying school and the kids in school, and, as far as I knew, so were Lina and Mike.

The school was having a Halloween celebration the last school day of October. My father was tired; they had a bad day on the farm. I begged him to take us to the Halloween party at school. I had a great time dunking for apples and trying to pin the tail on the donkey. I got into every game; I had the best time ever that night in my whole eight years of existence. I would be eight next month, on November 25. Little did I know by the time I would be eight I would no longer be here. I would have traded that night for anything in the world, just to leave us alone (my father, Tony, my sister Lina, my brother Mike, and me) and let us live our lives the way we were.

People have no right to come into a household and tell you how you should live your life, as long as you are not breaking any laws.

Before the week was up, some women from the social workers' department paid a visit to our house. It seems at the Halloween party it was discovered that this man was raising three children without a mother to care for them. In their opinion this was impossible. They convinced my father it would be best for the children to go elsewhere, or they scared him into agreeing, and maybe it would be a load off his back. They said it was just to make sure we got an education and we could come home in the summer. They came the week before Thanksgiving. Lina and Mike were ready to go—I wouldn't go. They said, "We want you to have a nice Thanksgiving dinner, turkey, apple pie, ice cream, candy." They promised everything, a playground with swings, sliding board, you name it.

I said, "I know you are lying. They can't have everything you say."

"It is there just waiting for you," they said.

"I want to spend my birthday at home."

Well, they were surprised and wanted to know when it was. I told them the twenty-fifth of November. It was a few days away from Thanksgiving. They wanted to know if they could come. I said, "Yes, but you will have to bring something; we don't have anything." They did come and they brought the cake, ice cream, and candy. It was the first birthday that I remembered. It was a nice day and I was nice, too.

They came to get us after Thanksgiving. I still did not want to go. They tried to drag me to the car. Tony tried to talk me into going. They wanted Tony to make me get into the car or force me in. I broke free from the lady who was holding onto me and climbed one of the big apple trees in the yard. They tried to coax me down. Tony went and got a ladder; he put it into the tree near me. I told Tony, with a firm voice, "Don't you come up here." From the tone of my voice I'm sure my father thought it best not to force me. He said I would have to come down on my own. Tony left the women there with me. He went back to work in the barn. I stayed in the tree all day with the women taking turns trying to coax me out of the tree. Mike, Lina, and Tony came a few times, asking me to come down. I was having a hard time (with me); I was happy (right there). The unknown I was uneasy with. As far as I knew, I did not want anything else.

It was now well after dark. I was cold and hungry. I finally gave in and came down. I was mad at myself for giving in. They told me what I had to do, and I did as I was told, like a trained dog. As we left, I saw my father standing there so humble and sad. At that time I was mad at him. I don't know what was going on in his mind then. Later on, when I remembered him standing there, I figured it wasn't pleasant.

The social worker took us to the city of Port Jervis, New York, on the border of Pennsylvania and New Jersey, to a Catholic orphanage. There were about eighty children there from about five to sixteen years old.

I was lonely; from what I don't know. In here there was something going on all the time, eighty kids running around, fighting, crying, laughing, like a bunch of animals in a cage. That's it! The cage! I was caged in! We were fenced in; you could not go out of the yard, which in size was about 100 by 130 feet with two-by-four foot slabs of bluestone covering the ground. The only thing here that they had promised was the swings; there wasn't another toy in the yard.

I would stand by the eight-foot-high Cyclone fence and watch the other kids outside on the street and sidewalk playing. No one ever came or played on our side of the street or sidewalk. Sometimes the kids outside would stop and stare at me. In a few days I realized it was me staring at them. It was real hard for me; my freedom was gone. I could not do what I wanted to do. It was like being in boot camp, but I didn't know it then. When I got to boot camp this place came to mind. Lina and Mike seemed to be happy. I started to wet the bed. I did not do it on purpose; I just couldn't help it. I was sulking for days. I was doing awful in school; the nuns put me back with the kids in second grade. I would not participate with the kids in third grade. Everyone in my third-grade class was from a home outside the orphanage. I would not do any homework, either.

Grandma and Grandpa, with Tony, came to visit us around Christmastime. Grandma grabbed the three of us, Lina, Mike, and me, in her arms and she cried. She held us in her arms, saying things in Italian and kissing us. As I looked at Tony and Grandpa, they had tears in their eyes. I'm sure it was something good Grandma was saying. The presents my grandparents gave us on that visit we never saw again. The nuns took them. I don't know what they were. When the children in the orphanage ripped their clothing, the nuns would get a new or used item from the storeroom. Every time I would see a new item given to a child I wondered if it was ours. For Christmas at the orphanage we had fruit, cookies, and ice cream on Christmas Day. No one got any gifts.

The Christmas in 1937 was the same.

When school started after the Christmas holidays I asked the nun to put me back in the third grade. They let me back in third grade, and by Easter time I was passing my grades. I graduated to fourth grade in June 1937. There were a lot of incidents that happened while Lina, Mike, and I were in the orphanage, from Thanksgiving 1936 to June 1938 (nineteen months).

Every once in a while a couple, man and wife, would visit the orphanage and spend an hour or two watching the children play. I got nervous when this happened and would find my brother and sister and stand guard over them. The couple was there looking to adopt a child. I did not want us to be separated. Or was it I didn't want to be left alone? I didn't make myself lovable in front of these people as so many kids did. We went through all the usual childhood diseases, measles, mumps, chicken pox, one cold after another, and we all had boils. They just wouldn't go away.

In the month of March, before Easter of 1938, I became seriously ill. I don't know what I had, but I lost a lot of weight. I became skin and bones; I was delirious. I think I had typhoid fever. I had a fever; I don't know how high. They filled a tub with ice water. I was put in a tub of very hot water for a while, then in cold water, or vice versa, for a while. The nuns did this in their quarters. (There was not a tub in the area where we children were housed. We would line up by ten sinks and wash ourselves with washcloths. The kid behind you would wash your back.) The nuns would try to get me in the cold water to bring my temperature down to break the fever I had. I resisted. Finally, a couple more nuns came and they were able to force me into the tub and held me under the water, except my head. Well, I must have called them everything but Holy of Holies. I must have cursed in Italian, too.

When I woke up, there was a nun by the side of the bed I was in, changing towels, trying to cool my body with ice water. I said I was hungry. For the first time since I'd been at the orphanage, I saw the nuns smile and laugh. I could not believe it. I was in the bed of the one nun who was friendly when I woke up. I had been delirious for three days. The nuns had around a seventy-hour vigil watching over me. After the nun brought me something to eat, she had to feed me, as I could not raise my arms.

While feeding me she wanted to know how I knew so many bad words. I had a grin on my face, I think. When I looked in the mirror all I saw was skin and teeth. The nun said, "It is not funny. Sister [so and so; I don't know her name] is Italian. She wanted to push your head under the water. She said a boy so rotten inside should not live." The nun asked where I learned such words. I said I was with men all the time. "And the Italian ones?" she asked.

I said, "My father."

The nun just shook her head. This nun would sleep in a chair for another week until I could get around. Every day they made me walk up and down the halls in the section the nuns lived in, plain, bare rooms with just the necessities to survive. Soon I was able to go back with the others and resume my duties and go back to school.

Tony would come to see us every three or four months while we were in the orphanage. When he came to visit that Easter (1938) I was just over my illness. I was gaunt and had boils on my feet, legs, and back. Lina and Mike didn't look much better. Tony brought candy and cookies. The nuns took them and when Tony went to leave I whispered in his ear, "Pa, if you don't get us out of here soon we are all going to be dead by the time you come again."

Tony said, "I'll do something."

31

I passed fourth grade in June 1938. The last weekend after school was out, Tony and Mr. Blank came to visit us. After half an hour or so Tony wanted to take us out to an ice-cream store. The nuns said it would spoil our supper. Tony said, "I'll have them back for supper." He said to us kids, "Come on; we are going," ignoring what the nun was saying. We left and got into the back of a pickup truck that belonged to Mr. Blank. A couple of the nuns stood in the doorway, and as we went up the street in Port Jervis the nuns waved at us; I waved back. They knew we were not coming back, just as I knew. In about five minutes we were out of town on a country road. Lina and Mike wanted to know how long it would be before we would get to the ice-cream store. My father was looking out the back window of the pickup with a smile on his face. I smiled back and enjoyed the ride home. This was June of 1938. I was nine and a half years old.

5

Things Looked Better; That's All

We came to Mr. Blank's farm in the town of Gardiner, New York. The farm Tony worked on when we went to the orphanage had been sold to the federal government. They were building an airport.

We had no clothes and very little furniture in the house. There was a bed in each of the three bedrooms upstairs and a table, three chairs, and a big cast-iron stove in the kitchen. Oh, there was a well outside for water and an outhouse. Tony had to go to work; we were to wait at the house until he came home. The main house, which Mr. Blank lived in, was about a quarter of a mile away, and the barn was nearby. Mr. Blank had sixty milking cows, a dozen or so other cows, and a team of horses that Tony used to work the farm. The farm had 320 acres of fields, woods, pasture, and apple orchard.

Tony came home about 7:00 P.M. with a stainless-steel pail half-full of milk. We had bread and milk for our first supper in our new home. I don't know about anyone else, but I felt good. I was free and happy. Tony got up at four in the morning and went to work to milk the cows and do the other chores, then came home for breakfast with some eggs and some more milk. We had eggs, bread, and milk for breakfast. Later that day Mr. Blank took us to Gardiner to shop, and while my father bought supplies Mr. Blank took us kids to an ice-cream parlor. We had our ice cream.

When we came home and put the supplies away, everything was dried stuff or in cans or sacks. We had no electricity or icebox; we lived on a dirt road. The town we just came back from was about seven miles away.

After a few days, when Tony got up at four in the morning I got up and asked if I could go with him to work. He said I had to watch Lina and Mike. (Maggie was still in the hospital, and Tony, Jr., was still at Grandma's, and Helen was still living with Mrs. White.) I said, "They will sleep until we come home for breakfast," and that started the early-morning rising for me.

I got up every morning, and on the way home for breakfast Tony and I would plan the day for me. We had a garden that had to be weeded; there was an empty chicken coop that had to be fixed up so we could get some chickens. Tony didn't always come home for lunch; if they worked on the other end of the farm, they didn't come in for lunch. I would start cooking around 5:00 P.M. with instructions that Tony gave me, telling me what to do. In the summer I used a little kerosene stove.

After doing the chores that had to be done, Lina and Mike would play by the house, and each day I would venture farther and farther from the house. I found wild strawberries. The next day I brought Lina and Mike with me and we ate and picked the berries. We would have them in the morning with our cereal.

A couple of days after we were home from the orphanage, one evening after supper we were playing with Tony and he started to itch and scratch himself. He grabbed my head, and looked in my hair, then Lina's hair and Mike's hair. Then he rattled off a string of cusswords in Italian and a few in English; we had head lice. That was another problem they had in the orphanage. The next night when Tony came home from work he brought the hand clippers that they used on the horses and cows from the barn. Tony cut all of our hair off and I cut his all off, and we burned the hair. The boils I had were healing. I was feeling better each day.

One night soon after we came home from the orphanage, Tony came home with a twelve-gauge shotgun. I asked, "What is that for?" and he said, "To shoot rats." I never saw any rats. A few months later it casually came out that the gun was to fend off anyone who came to take us away. As I got a little older and bigger, I started to shoot the gun. This was the gun that I did a lot of hunting with.

Mr. Blank had a housekeeper who had a son a little younger than Mike. Most of the summer Mike stayed with the housekeeper's son, Malcolm, and Lina spent much of the day with the housekeeper. Every night at suppertime Lina would give us the news of the neighborhood. I don't know where they got the news from. There was no electricity, no phones, and the nearest neighbor was a quarter-mile away.

After breakfast I would go with Tony to work. Sometimes I could not go for the type of work being done in the field. If he was mowing, cultivating, or spreading manure, I could not go. On those days I would go off by myself. One day I went to a chicken farm about a quarter-mile from home. Mr. Peterson had five thousand chickens. He asked me many questions about me and my family. When I went home that evening he gave me two chickens that had died while laying eggs and a dozen eggs. This happened frequently. I asked him why he did not eat them. He said, "We do. The chickens are good for food. We have chicken two to three times a week. Most of the time I throw them away. In a couple of days I'll have a few more." Every couple of days I would go to the

Peterson farm. I would offer to help with the chores for payment for the chickens. On the days he didn't have any chickens I went home with eggs. Some days we worked really hard and he would give me what change he had in his pocket, plus the two chickens and eggs. The change would be from sixty to ninety-five cents. I was almost ten at this time. I gave the money to my father.

One day Mr. Peterson asked if I had a vaccination mark on me somewhere. I said I didn't know. He looked me over and said, "I don't see any." Mr. Peterson asked if my brother and sister were vaccinated. I said no. Mr. Peterson was going to Gardiner to the three-room school. They were vaccinating children for free at the school the next day. He said he would take us to town. I was to ask my father. On looking me over, Mr. Peterson wanted to know what I had in my shoes. I wore just a pair of pants; we didn't have any socks, either. I didn't wear a shirt all summer. The cow feed came in a linen sack. After it was empty the cloth could be used for making something or sewn together to make sheets. Tony cut the sacks into squares about eighteen by eighteen inches. You would put your foot in it, fold it over, and slip your foot into your shoe; those were our socks. I said to Tony that night at supper that Lina, Mike, and I were going to the Gardiner school to get vaccinated or we could not go to school and it was free. Tony gave me fifty cents to buy two tins of half-and-half tobacco, and that was that.

Next morning Mr. and Mrs. Peterson, with their baby, came to pick us up on the way to Gardiner. About three miles from our house, just before we came to a hard-surfaced road, there was a one-room schoolhouse that we would be going to in a couple of weeks. We went on for another four miles to Gardiner. In town they had a three-room school, grades 1 and 2 in one room, 3 and 4 in one of the other rooms, and 5 and 6 in the last room. After sixth grade a bus took you to New Paltz School for seventh grade on to high school. That trip was about ten miles from Gardiner.

Lina got her vaccination in the thigh so you would not see a scar on her arm; the boys, it did not matter. Mr. Peterson stopped to get us ice-cream cones, and I got two cans of half-and-half tobacco for Tony. We started home and there was a sharp turn in town. As we went around the turn the car door on Lina's side flew open and Lina fell out. I was on the other side. I pushed Mike out of the way and grabbed Lina and hollered, "Stop the car!" I held onto Lina and we dragged her about fifty feet before Mr. Peterson stopped the car. People on the side of the road said if I had not grabbed Lina, she would have been run over by the car's rear wheel. Lina's leg was scraped pretty badly but she had no broken bones. Mr. Peterson was pretty broken up over the incident. Lina still had her ice-cream cone in her hand, and she smiled at Mr. Peterson when he picked her up and put her back into the car. He looked a little relieved when he got behind the wheel and drove home.

By the time school started Lina was healing very well, with the help of tit balm, a salve (ointment) we used on the cows' udders.

6

Getting an Education, More Ways Than One

When school started in September 1938, I didn't get up with Tony on school days. I made breakfast and helped Lina and Mike get ready for school. I made peanut-butter-and-jelly sandwiches; we used the wax paper from the cereal boxes for wrapping our sandwiches and saved the wax paper and paper bag to use over again. We walked to school. School started at 9:00 A.M. and went to 3:00 P.M. The school was one room, forty feet wide and fifty feet long, one front door, a coat closet to the right, a wood storage area on the left, and a big cast-iron potbelly stove in the middle of the room. There were six rows of desks, three rows on each side of the stove, five desks in each row. From left, first grade, second row, second grade, and so on to the sixth row, sixth grade. If all the desks were full, the school could hold thirty children. There were seventeen children in school that year (1938), one in the first grade, none in the second grade, four in the third grade, six in the fourth grade, four in the fifth grade (including me), and two in the sixth grade.

Our teacher was a young woman just out of college from New Paltz, which was a state teachers' college. Miss Moran had lived in Gardiner all her life, so she was not far from home. We started school barefoot, Lina, Mike, and myself. Tony had ordered shoes for us, but they hadn't come in yet. We had only one change of clothes, and they were rags. We wore our school clothes all week, and on Saturday or Sunday we washed them "if they needed it or not." The three of us needed a haircut, and we needed a little grooming. We were scraggly and scrawny. (When I look back and remember what we looked like, we must have looked like we lived in a cave.)

Miss Moran could not understand it; here these three kids are so unkempt (we probably looked like animals of some sort) and they are the smartest ones in the school. That was a quote I heard Miss Moran say to any adult whenever one would stop to visit her. I guess the Catholic schooling in the orphanage gave us an edge. The oldest student there was Harold. He was just waiting to be sixteen to stay home and work on his father's farm. He was in the sixth grade. Harold took care of the stove in the winter and went to the neighbor's for drinking water every day.

I have to make this observation—I must have had extraordinary hearing. Adults (they have reached maturity) would talk about a child in hearing range of that child. I have never understood that. Sometimes it would be complimentary, and other times it would be demeaning. Either way, if it's to be a secret, keep it a secret.

A couple of weeks after school started, Miss Moran said she had some clothes to give us and would take us home. When we unloaded the car and put the box of clothes on the porch, Miss Moran asked to see our mother. I said, "She isn't here; she is in the hospital." Miss Moran asked, "Anything serious?"

I said, "She needs some rest." (That's what I was always told.)

The clothes did not fit, either too small or too big; we made use of them.

I enjoyed school. As Miss Moran would be teaching a couple of kids in third or fourth grade, we in the other grades would be studying for our turn to be quizzed by Miss Moran. On occasion she would be asking a child over and over for an answer and I would give it. Miss Moran would scold me, "Henry, you can't keep doing this."

I said, "When you keep asking the same question over and over, it breaks my concentration and I can't study."

Once in a while Miss Moran would have me tutor one of the lower grades. I had to get my homework done in school. After school I had chores to do and did not have time for homework.

We had very cold weather and a lot of snow that winter (1938–39). We had a snowstorm that lasted three days. It was so bad, you couldn't go anywhere. The snow was too deep; the roads were closed. The farmers had to throw the milk away for two days. The snowdrifts piled up in the roads. Some places the snow was eight feet deep in the roads; average depth in most of the roads was four feet. All the farmers in the area had to get the sleds out and use the horses to go through the fields from farm to farm cutting fences to get the milk to the creamery. It would be an all-day trip. There was no school for a week. Everything hinged on keeping warm and keeping the food supply up. Most of that winter we slept in the kitchen. It was fifteen by twenty feet in size. When we went to school no one was in the house all day, so we let the fire go out. I would build a fire in the stove when I came home from school.

The people in the area were kind to us. They were always giving us something. Thanksgiving time there was a bushel basket of all kinds of goodies and a turkey on the front porch the morning before Thanksgiving.

There was a big old farmhouse halfway to school that had burned almost to the ground. One little section by a big stone chimney was intact. The farm was abandoned by the owners. Mr. Newkirk rented the fields from the owners; they lived in New York City. They would come up once a year. Every now and then we would see a man in the middle of the burned-out house. It was said the house was haunted and everyone would stay away. Coming home from school one day, I saw smoke coming from the chimney of the burned-out house. I went up the hill a short distance to the house. In the center of the house was a path from one end of the house to the other end, where the piece that hadn't burned stood. I knocked on the door; a man came to the door. Every time I met an adult for the first time he wanted to know who I was and where I lived; I was ready with the answers. Then it was my turn; we talked a few minutes. This man was a trapper; he had fixed the room so one could live in it. He had animal skins all over the place. I would stop afterward to see him. Sometimes he would be skinning an animal; I would watch.

Near the end of the winter, February and March (1939), Mr. Peterson was having a section of his woods logged for the timber. The men set up a sawmill, just a table to hold the logs in place and a big engine on a wagon to run the saw. They took the wheels off the wagon and leveled and braced the engine. The saw was run by a large belt. On Saturdays I would bring drinking water to the men working the mill. They squared the logs; they sawed the bark off and made the logs square. The pieces they cut off were called slabs. After cutting the logs they would cut the slabs up in small pieces to be sold as firewood. The men took a break and drank some of the fresh water I had just brought to the work site. They were getting ready to finish the day's work by cutting up the slabs. One of the men went to the saw blade that was about four feet in diameter and turning at a very high speed. He bent down to clear some bark that lay under the turning saw blade. The two getting the slabs stopped and watched as the man went for the pieces of bark. The other man came up behind me, grabbed me really tight, and put one hand over my mouth, and he whispered really softly but clearly and precisely, "Do . . . not . . . say . . . a . . . word," in my ear. At that point blood started to fly and drop on the snow. The man pulled back; he put his hand on the side of his head and said something (I don't know what). One man went to the man at the saw; the man who had held me went to the pickup truck. The man, after turning the saw off, started looking in the sawdust; he found the ear that had been cut off, and washed it in the pail of drinking water. Then he went over and placed the ear back on the man who had lost it, blood all over the place. The three of them got into the back of the pickup. As they drove off, I heard one man say, "It's thirty miles," and the other one said, "Leave it there; it's stopping the bleeding." Those were the first words spoken by the four men in that three or four minutes. They all knew what to do, as if they had done this before. The hospital was in Kingston, New York, and about thirty miles away.

I took the belt off the saw and engine. I rolled it up, drained the water out of the engine like they did, and covered the engine and saw with the canvas like they did; everything looked neat. I took the water pail home and washed it and the dipper. It was dark and very late when the men got back from the hospital. They went out to the woods to drain the engine and cover things up and saw it was done. They went to thank Mr. Peterson; they figured I had told him what happened. Mr. Peterson told them he was sorry about the mishap. He said, "Henry didn't come by tonight. He was probably running late. He has chores to do at home and has to start supper for his father and brother and sister."

On Sunday morning I went to the Peterson farm to see if he had any chickens for Sunday dinner. I told him what had happened, and he told me his story. I went home with a couple of chickens and eggs after I helped him draw water for the chickens. The men were back on the job on Monday morning; I could hear the engine running in the woods on the way to school. They would be gone by the time I got home from school. I had to wait until Saturday to find out anything. In the meantime we had to cut wood for our stove. On Sundays, Tony, Mike, and I would cut a couple of dead trees down in the woods in back of our house, then cut them into ten- to fourteen-foot lengths, according to the size that two of us boys could carry home on our shoulders to the cellar. Every night after supper we would cut wood for the stove. After my morning chores at home that following Saturday I couldn't wait to get to Mr. Peterson and help him with the chickens. I really wanted to know what happened with the man and his ear.

Mr. Peterson knew it, too. After we had lunch at his house he said to me, "Take some drinking water out to the loggers." The four loggers were there; they all came up to me as soon as they saw me with the water. I looked at the man who got his ear cut with the saw. He had sliced a thin layer of flesh off part of his face, too. His ear was on a little crooked. He wanted to give me four dollars and thanked me for looking after his machine. I said I did not want the money. All four of them insisted I take the money. Then I said, "How much firewood could I buy with the four dollars?"

The men looked at one another. The man with the crooked ear said, "One load."

I said, "OK." Late in the day they loaded the pickup with the cut slabs and I showed them where I lived.

Later Mr. Peterson said to me, "You are going to do all right in the world."

I said, "What do you mean?"

"One day you will know."

I never thought or remembered what he said until I got to this part of the story I'm writing right now, 9:20 P.M., on March 21, 2000. You know something? I am doing all right! (I can't believe this.)

My brother Mike was happy as could be when he saw the pile of cut-up wood. My father, Tony, was all smiles when he saw the wood in the front yard.

That following week a man from Poughkeepsie came to the woods looking for work at the sawmill. They said they didn't need any help. He begged them to let him work for the day. They said OK. From what I was told, early in the afternoon, while they were felling a tree, it kicked back and the trunk hit the worker in the stomach and buried him in the snow, killing him. I didn't hear about it until Saturday. Mr. Peterson told me when I came to help him with the chickens. I had wondered why I did not hear the engine on Thursday or Friday. They didn't know the man's last name, as he didn't have a driver's license. They put him in the car, and one of the men drove the car to the police station in Poughkeepsie. They found his family from the license plates. He had borrowed the car from a friend.

44

I asked Mr. Peterson how come the ear was stitched on crooked. He said riding in the back of the truck on the bumpy road they could not keep the ear straight. It was knitting and looked like it was healing well by the time they got to the hospital. The doctor looked at it and thought it best to stitch it the way it was. All agreed.

Mr. Peterson had a lot of iron traps hanging in his barn. I asked him what they were for. He used to trap for rats, but now he used the wooden type. I asked if I could borrow six of the traps. I said, "I saw a half-dozen holes in the ground that looked active."

He said, "Take all you want."

Monday on the way home from school I dropped in to see the trapper and told him I had gotten some traps from Mr. Patterson and if I caught something could I sell it to him? He said that a fur buyer came around every couple of weeks. The trapper's name was Mr. Stevens. He said I had to skin the animal and I should look at my traps twice a day. If I went only once a day or whenever I felt like it, I should not trap. The animal might be alive and should be killed as soon as possible, or a fox could come by and take the animal. I set the traps out so the run I made was like a horseshoe. I covered close to two miles. I used eight traps.

Tony got up at four-thirty in the morning, and he would wake me about five A.M. when he left the house for work. I would run my trapline, get back around six and start getting things ready for breakfast, and wake Lina and Mike to get ready for school. There were only a few weeks left to trap this season. I caught a raccoon, a possum, rabbits, skunks, weasels, and a squirrel. The squirrel almost finished my trapping career. The third or fourth day on my trapping run it was cold; the wind blowing really hard. The day before, I caught a rabbit. They are easy to kill. I was in a hurry to get in out of the cold. I came to one of the holes and something was pulling hard on the chain. It wouldn't come out. I reached in the hole, and a squirrel clamped its jaws on my ring finger on my right hand, near the back of my hand. I grabbed it with my left hand, around its neck, and pulled the squirrel. Although I did not realize it at the time, the pain in my finger was terrible. I pulled the squirrel with its teeth in each side of my finger. It cut a slit the full length of my finger on each side. There was not much left of it to eat; it was bait now, the blood all over the place in the snow. I cried all the way home, more for being stupid than from the pain. When I got home I cut strips of cloth from the feed sack and used the tit balm on my finger before I wrapped it up. Lina and Mike had to do breakfast and get the lunch ready.

I did not see Mr. Stevens all week. I wanted to tell him what happened. I could not wait around after school; I had to look after my traps and get home to do my chores.

Saturday Mr. Peterson wanted to know what had happened. I told him. He just said, "Hmmmm." We worked all morning, cleaning the roosting areas in some of the pens. After we ate lunch, Mr. Peterson came outside with a .22-caliber pump rifle and some bottles. He set them up on a rock about one hundred feet away, loaded the rifle, and shot and hit them one at a time. We put more bottles up. Mr. Peterson gave me some instructions on how to use the rifle and said, "Now you shoot." I shot three times before I hit one. He said, "That's all right; it will come. When you go on your trap run, take the gun, but only put one bullet in it. This way you won't get hurt or forget how many are left in the gun."

I was ten years and four months old at this time. I asked about buying the gun.

He said, "No! This is my favorite gun." He would order me one from Montgomery Ward's catalog. After we got done working that afternoon Mr. Peterson showed me the gun in the catalog that he would order for me. It would cost seventeen dollars. I would have to work seventeen Saturdays to pay it off. We shook hands on it. I always gave whatever money I earned to my father. I would keep a few dollars from the furs I sold to buy a couple of boxes of bullets. I did a lot of shooting with the .22. I was able to shoot a hickory nut in a tree. Thank God I was miles away from civilization. I missed many a nut.

7

How We Met Our Doctor

Things seemed to be going along normally until school was out. I passed fifth grade on into sixth grade in June 1939. One Sunday afternoon in early June, Lina, Mike, and I were playing in the front yard. A car with three people passed our house. (Weekends were the only time we would see a car or two.) This car stopped and backed up! A man came over to us and called to my sister, "Come here, little girl." He looked her over, went back to the car, and got a satchel. He said, "I'm a doctor. Show me the little girl's bedroom and tell your mother I'm here."

I told him, "My mom is in a hospital."

The doctor examined Lina, then said, "This girl is very sick. She has to stay in bed for a week, and you bring her food and water and make her use the potty." He said Lina had jaundice. (Lina was yellow.) Mike and I were red from being outside all of the time. At that age I thought nothing of it. The doctor said, "I will see you next week."

When Tony came home I told him what happened. Tony said, "They must be the people that bought the old Tookey farm across the road from Mr. Blank's house. What about school?"

I said, "Mike will stay home with Lina on Monday, and I will stay home on Tuesday."

I told Miss Moran that Lina was sick and had to stay in bed. We worked out a way Lina would stay home alone.

Lina wanted to sleep all the time, so it was no trouble to leave her alone. We had water by the bed. I emptied the potty and we would have something for her to eat by the bed. Lina wanted to know if she had passed fourth grade. Everybody in school had passed to the next grade. The doctor stopped the next weekend; he was very pleased with the progress Lina was making. He gave me more pills and said Lina didn't have to stay in bed anymore, but she could not play and run or do any work of any kind. She must rest. He told me his name was Dr. Boutzell, and in a few minutes of conversation I found out he did buy the old Tookey farm for a retreat. The buildings were in such bad shape, the roof leaked, windows were broken or gone, and the siding was falling off. The doctor had pitched a big tent on what was the lawn. He and his wife and daughter lived in the tent when they came up during the summer months. They had a little vegetable garden, and they would work on the old house; they wanted to restore it.

Tony got a hundred chicks through the mail from Montgomery Ward's. I fixed up the chicken coop; we kept the chicks in the other room in the house for a couple of weeks. When it got cold we would light a fire in the stove to keep the birds warm. When the weather got warmer they went out to the coop.

I was getting more work to do. Tony built a pigpen next to the chicken coop, and we got a little pig. Tony started a vegetable garden, too. We all worked in the garden. I had to feed and water the animals and clean the pens when necessary. I still had my agreement with Mr. Peterson. I enjoyed going to work for Mr. Peterson; Mrs. Peterson was a good cook. I ate like a king when I worked for him; sometimes I was given a piece of cake or pie to bring home.

We hadn't seen the doctor go by in a week or two. He might have come up during the night. It was the first weekend in August. I walked to the barn where Tony worked. When we got to the driveway to the Tookey farm I said, "I'll go see if anyone is home." No one had been there, it looked like (according to the height of the grass), for at least two weeks. I cut the grass with a push mower that was in the old house. I cut a few little saplings that had started to grow in the old lawn, and mowed some more grass. After I got done I went to the barn where Tony worked and told him no one had been there for a couple of weeks. I said I cut the grass. I said, "Pa, I'll see you later," and went home to do my chores. Our work around the house and garden was caught up. I asked Tony if it would be all right for me to weed the doctor's garden. I said, "The weeds have overgrown everything." The next two days when I had time I weeded the doctor's garden. I was very pleased with myself. Then I started to think maybe the doctor would not like the idea that I took the liberty to do this. He might not approve of me being here, period. I thought about cleaning out some of the debris in the house. I decided not to.

The Shawangunk Kill, a rather big stream or small river, was a half-mile away from the house. The river was the west/northwest boundary of Mr. Blank's farm for almost three-quarters of a mile. We would go fishing and swimming in the river quite often. One day Mike and I caught five big large-mouthed black bass. They went from twenty-two to twenty-eight inches in length. We felt so good about our catch that on the way home we stopped off at the barn. It was milking time. We showed our fish to Mr. Blank and my father. Mr. Blank could not get over the size of the fish. The farm had been in the Blanks' name for almost 300 years, going from father to son for years. The barn we stood in, in July 1939, was 200 years old. Never, to his knowledge, were any fish of any kind that big caught in the river. Mike and I went on home to clean the fish for supper. When Tony came home he said whenever we set a trap, hunt, or fish we should not bring our catch to the barn or tell anyone what we caught. Mr. Blank was so jealous and envious of us he just kept saying, "All night, I can't believe it. If I didn't see it with my own eyes, I wouldn't have believed it."

About a week later a friend of Mr. Blank came to the farm to visit and asked us about the fish we caught. Would I take him to the river and show him where I caught them? This man goes to his car; he put on a vest with all kinds of trinkets in it and hanging from it, a hat that had more stuff on it, all kinds of fishhooks with feathers on them.

A fish pole and reel, a fish net, can of worms, a jar of bugs—I never saw so much stuff that you use for fishing. The first thing I thought of was, *He is going to catch all the fish in the river. They don't have a chance.* Well, I took him to the river and to all the spots where we *never* caught any fish. He did not catch any fish, either. I said that I don't always catch fish when I fished.

That weekend the doctor came to the farm. He stopped by to thank me and wanted to give me some money. I said, "I don't want any money." He wanted to do something for me; I said, "That was for helping Lina. Thank you."

He said, "I still owe you," and I said, "I could use a box of twenty-two caliber bullets."

He said, "Next time I come up, you got them." He came up this time with only his wife. (It was hot.) The doctor was so happy the grass was cut and the garden was weeded and never looked better. He imagined himself working his ass off to catch up. He said, "Henry, can you take us to the river where you swim? I'm going to relax this weekend. This is the best weekend I've had in years." (Of course, I thought he was nuts at that time. I did not know what he was talking about.)

We all got into our swimsuits. The doctor and his wife had towels, hats, sunglasses, and a big bag that had lotion and a thermos bottle with water. The doctor saw the smirk on my face and said, "Henry, don't say anything." I took the bag of stuff from Mr. Boutzell ("boatsell" is the way it's pronounced). We started down Mr. Blank's driveway between the house and barn through a cow pasture, through an apple orchard, through a hay field, through a cornfield and another hay field, and then we could see the river winding and turning at the end of the hay field. I took them to the part of the river where it was very wide. It had a sandy beach on both sides, and the water was from four to six feet deep. It really was as tranquil and beautiful as the doctor's wife said. I guess that's why I liked it here, too.

Next, the doctor saw freshwater mussels all over the place. He said, "Henry, you never told me there were mussels in the river."

I said, "So?"

The doctor said they were good to eat. Lina, Mike, and I played in the water for short periods, then lay on the towels for a while.

After a while I asked the doctor if he would like to have a fish for supper. He said, "Could you?" I said yes. I went downstream and turned over a few rocks and got a hellgrammite for bait. Then I went to a hollow in a tree on the bank and got my ball of string with a hook and a wine bottle cork for a bob. I went upstream. There was a tree lying halfway across the stream. The roots were in the middle of the stream, with deep water on each side of the tree. I would climb out on the roots and throw the cork and hellgrammite upstream and let it flow downstream as far as my line could go, pull it back, and do it again and again. Sometimes my line got tangled. It would take a few minutes to untangle it. Before fifteen minutes were up I caught a nice-sized large-mouth bass. I took it to shore and broke a branch off of a little bush with a Y in it. I put the fish on it and stuck the branch with the fish on it in the bank under the water to keep the fish alive until we went home.

As I straightened up, I saw the doc standing on the top of the bank. He said, "Henry, you are a good fisherman. I would like you and your brother to help gather up some of these mussels."

We took everything out of the rattan wicker bag and rolled it up in the towels. We put as many mussels as the doc could carry in the bag. Lina and Mike each had a towel with stuff in it. I had the fish and some mussels in a towel over my shoulders, and Mrs. Boutsell had all she could do to bring herself. When we got to Doc's place he asked us to stay and taste the mussels. I said Lina and Mike could stay; I had to go home and do chores and start supper for Tony. Lina and Mike came home with more pills and medicine.

The next weekend Doc gave me 500 rounds of ammo, ten boxes of .22 caliber bullets. He also gave me a bamboo fishing pole, fishing line, hooks, and a couple of bobs. He said he didn't bring a reel because you can't leave a reel in a tree; it would rust. I kept saying, "Thank you." The doctor kept saying what a nice weekend they had last weekend.

He wanted us to do him a favor. He took two five-gallon pails out of his trunk. Could we fill them up for him with the mussels by Sunday night when he went back to the city? We did.

8

What a Surprise For All

The next weekend on Sunday, Labor Day weekend in September, Tony, Lina, Mike, and I were all working together fixing Sunday dinner, the only day when there was time to fuss with a meal. We had from 9:00 A.M. or so to about 4:00 P.M. before we had to do our chores, taking care of the animals again. A car pulled up in our front yard; we went to the door in bewilderment. I recognized Grandpa and Grandma; with them were Uncle John and Maggie (Mom) and my brother Tony, Jr. (six years old now). I had not seen Tony, Jr., for three years plus. I did not recognize him. I knew it had to be Tony, Jr.; who else could it be? Uncle John was more of a stranger then, too. I don't know if Tony (Pa) knew they were coming or not. Lina, Mike, and I didn't know. The mailbox was three miles away where the dirt road meets the macadam road. Mr. Blank would drive out for the mail once a week. If Tony got mail we never knew. Grandma had gotten Maggie out of the hospital near the end of May. Maggie lived with Grandma and Tony, Jr., all summer, at least three months, to get acclimated to domestic life. Grandma had electric lights, steam heat, running water, hot or cold, very comfortable conditions, a radio, telephone, and her pantry overflowing with foodstuffs. What a surprise this must have been to see how we were living, for Tony Jr.

We put more plates on the table. Grandpa had brought a gallon of his homemade wine; he made three to four hundred gallons of wine a year. I remember them making it the year I lived there. Grandma brought vegetables from her garden. We unloaded the clothes for Maggie and Tony, Jr. The women took over the cooking; I kept running to the well for water. We ate, one sitting, one standing, whatever—we only had four chairs. Tony had to go to work at four. Grandma and Grandpa stayed a little while longer before they went home.

Mike and I were showing Tony, Jr. the pig, the chickens, and the pond in back of the house with frogs in it. We told Tony, Jr. not to tell Maggie about the frogs.

Tony, Jr. said, "You mean Mom?"

I thought for a few seconds and said, "Yeah, Mom." (I had become friends with the frogs! Of course, they knew that.) We stayed outside until Tony came home from work. Lina stayed in the house with her newfound mom. We picked and snacked on the leftover food and talked, getting acquainted all over again until bedtime. We had one more day before school started. Tony Jr., had not started school yet.

We had new shoes to start school this year; we went barefoot most of the summer. It was hard to get used to the shoes.

When we started school (1939) Tony, Jr. was in first grade, Mike in third, Lina in fourth, and I was in sixth grade.

I was the oldest in school this year, as three of the older boys had quit; they were sixteen years old. A couple of families moved away, and three new kids came to school plus Tony, Jr.

I inherited the job of getting the drinking water at the nearest farm and, when the mornings were cold, made a fire in the wood stove. After Halloween we needed the stove on all day. I asked for and got the key to the school so when I got there early in the morning I would have the school warm by school time. School was out at 3:15 P.M., so 2:00 P.M. would be about the last time wood was put in the stove.

Before Thanksgiving another two boys started school, one in the fifth grade named Walter and Herby in the sixth grade with me. Herby and I would study and ask each other questions. We more or less taught each other our lessons. Miss Moran would give us a test every Friday. On occasion Herby or I would help the younger children with their lessons.

9

Lost a Good Friend

Here it was trapping time again. I set out a dozen traps
this year on my run. I was a good shot with my .22 now.
Sometimes on my run in the morning or late afternoon I
would shoot an animal that was not in my traps, like
a fox or weasel. A weasel was hard to catch in a trap.
Occasionally I would shoot a rabbit. I would check in with
Mr. Stevens now and then. One Sunday morning I ran
into him on my trap line checking my traps and he
showed me how to trap for muskrat in the river.

Mom didn't get up in the morning with us. We kids
got up, got our own breakfast, and made our own lunches
like we did before Mom came to live with us. And now
we had Tony, Jr., to show and help teach the routine.
Tony, Jr., was stubborn; he would not wash up in the
morning or evening. He daydreamed most of the day in
school. He kept to himself most of the time. I mentioned
this to my father, Tony. I thought maybe Tony, Jr., was
sick or something was wrong. Tony said, "He will be all
right in a couple of weeks; he is lonely." It wasn't until
years later that I knew what was bothering Tony, Jr. He
came from a house with comfort, and Grandma was a
loving woman. She babied and pampered him. Now he
had chores to do like the rest of us. We all had to pull
our own weight. Thank God Mom got out of bed sometime
during the day and cooked supper. That meant I had a

little freedom for myself. I could take my time in the afternoon, when I would check my traps. I could hunt and look for a better place to set my traps. Mom was a very good cook with what we had, and with a few spices Mom made the food delicious. My stuff just filled a hungry hole in your stomach.

I had not seen Mr. Stevens the past week. One Saturday afternoon as I was looking after my traps and hunting, off in the distance I saw something big hanging from a large oak tree. I had a funny feeling about it. I wanted to look closer at it, but I could not go any closer. It wasn't far from the place where Mr. Stevens lived, next to Mr. Webster's farm. I didn't go near the tree. I went to Mr. Webster's house about a half-mile away up on top of a little hill. The word around was Mr. Webster was not very friendly. Everyone in the area would say, "Don't go on Mr. Webster's farm; he doesn't like people."

This is the first time I met Mr. Webster. He said, "How are you, Henry?"

I was surprised he knew my name. I said, "Mr. Webster, there is something big hanging in that big oak down in your woods."

"Oh, my God," he said. "Come into the house."

He talked a few minutes with his wife and went back outside. I started to follow him.

Mrs. Webster said, "You stay here, son. Put your gun in the corner by the door." She made some tea, and I had a piece of apple pie. When I was done, Mrs. Webster said, "You go on home now."

I said I would, and I did. I told Tony and the rest of the family at suppertime what had happened. Tony said he had heard about Mr. Stevens hanging himself. Why? He had an incurable disease. I said, "Mr.Webster seemed nice." Tony said, "He is? Why all the talk then?"

Tony said, "The electric company wants to bring an electric line up this road and everyone has to promise to be hooked up to buy power. Mr. Webster is the only one that doesn't want electric power, so everyone is mad at him."

Between running my trapline, taking care of the fire at school, getting fresh water for drinking for the day at school, doing my schoolwork, and taking care of the animals, I was busy. I was glad when we finally butchered the pig. I had to shoot the pig between the eyes with my .22 so as to stun the animal so it could be butchered. The pig weighed over three hundred pounds. Tony saved just about everything from the pig; we made sausage and smoked some. It was cold weather; the fresh meat hung in the smokehouse to protect it from the elements and wild animals. We ate fresh pork every day until it was all gone. After the pork was gone we had chickens for meat. In the middle of February 1940, we butchered a young steer—same scenario, shooting it between the eyes and butchering it. We ate beef every day until it was gone. We butchered the big animals in the winter months and saved the chickens, ducks, and geese for use for food in the hot months.

10

A Few New Comforts

We got electricity and I got more work. The electric company had men digging holes for the poles along the road. They started before school was let out in the spring of 1940. There were four men; they worked all summer and all fall before they got all the electric poles in the ground. Everything was done by hand, and they had to blast over half of the holes because of rock. There the poles stood without wire for over a year. It was early 1942 before we had electricity on the road and another three months to install power in our house.

In the summer of 1941 Tony dug a trench from the well to the kitchen and installed a hand pump inside the house by the sink. We didn't have to go outside for water anymore, so it didn't matter if it was raining or colder than hell out there. We still had to raise the pump handle and let the water drain back to the well in the winter months. It still got cold enough in the house at night to freeze the pipes and pump, so we had to prime the pump in the morning after the fire was started.

Everybody graduated to the next grade in the one-room schoolhouse in June 1940. That meant I would be going to New Paltz this fall for seventh grade.

Tony got another piglet to raise. Mr. Peterson was a carpenter by trade. He got a good offer to run a big job somewhere. He sold his chickens and gave us a couple dozen. Dr. Boutzell started coming up to his farm almost every weekend that summer. I started helping the doc gut the old house. We would work together on weekends. Before he went back to the city he would instruct me on what I could do while he was gone. The doc gave me three or four dollars when he came up to the farm plus candy and other goodies. It took the whole summer to gut the house. It looked good with just the studs standing. It was a big eight-room house, with nine-foot ceilings. Of course I was still able to take time off for fishing and swimming with my brothers. Sometimes Mike and Tony, Jr., would come with me to the doc's after we got our chores done at home. I would split the candy with them, which I did anyway.

We boys were always doing something outside. Mom and Lina, mostly Lina did everything inside. Now and then if we boys were home Lina would come out and play with us. She would at times ask us to stay home so she could play with us. We kids did most of the housework. Saturday or Sunday we would wash the clothes by hand. Up until the time the pump got put into the house I used to carry the water from the well to the stove to be heated up. This summer went by really fast. Before I knew it, it was Labor Day weekend again. Tony, Jr., and Mom had been here a year. Tony, Jr., was still sulking, though not as bad as he was in the earlier months.

Walking the three miles to school each morning, Malcolm would tease Tony, Jr., who was always in a sullen mood, pouting all the time. Most of the abuse from Malcolm was verbal. I would tell Tony, Jr. to fight back, say something, to no avail. I gave up trying to make Tony, Jr. fight. When Malcolm got too rough, I told him to knock it off and Malcolm would stop. The next year I went to New Paltz school, which meant I left for school an hour earlier to catch the school bus. Malcolm continued tormenting Tony, Jr. on their way to school. Tony, Jr. finally had it and struck Malcolm and then Tony, Jr. started to teasing and hurting Malcolm. Mike tried to make Tony, Jr. stop being so nasty. Mike asked me to talk to Tony, Jr. I said "Hey, it took Tony, Jr. a long time to defend himself". I told Tony, Jr. not to be so hard on Malcolm. It did not help. About a week later, Malcolm came to the Dondas's farm where I was working and started to beg me to make Tony, Jr. stop hitting him.

"Why should I? You would not stop when I told you to. What makes you think he will stop if I tell him to? I'm not going to beat him, it took him a long time to fight back. I'll tell you what I told Tony, Jr., when someone picks on you, fight back. You may get hurt in the fight, but then it's over. No one likes to get hurt every day."

The next day, Tony, Jr. and Malcolm got into a fist fight and drew blood on each other. Mike had to break it up. They did not tease each other anymore, and as time went on and they got older, they became good friends.

I had to leave the house earlier in the morning now to catch a bus that would be at the intersection by the one-room school at ten minutes to eight in the morning. Mike and another boy took over taking care of the stove and getting the drinking water. They got a coal stove and coal that year (1940). I was never in New Paltz before. The school was three stories high, three grades per floor, fourteen to sixteen rooms per floor. There were over twelve hundred children from first grade to ninth grade. The children came from the whole countryside. The school was a teachers' college. We would have a new teacher every six weeks. Our homeroom had a permanent teacher. There were also supervisors of the student teachers. I enjoyed school; these student teachers were full of energy and alive. Everything in class was a debate of a verbal discussion. I did well in school. We were given homework. I was able to get enough knowledge from the class so that I did my homework in school. We had one or two study classes a day. The only homework that had to be in every day was math, and that came very easily to me.

There were ninety-some kids in seventh grade, thirty-something in each of three rooms. The room I was in had six or seven boys who were waiting to turn sixteen. As a matter of fact, three turned sixteen in November before Thanksgiving and left school.

I didn't have time to run my trapline in the morning; I would run it at night. I was friendly with all the farmers in the area and set the trap line so it was on the way to or from school or on the way home. I missed Mr. Stevens that winter. I had no one to tell my experiences to or give me advice. The fur buyer still came around, not as often. After taking care of animals at night, as it got dark I would light a lantern and Mike, Tony, Jr., and I would go down into the cellar and cut wood for the stove until Tony came home for supper.

11

Who Was Killing Whom?

My father bartered with Mr. Blank over a cow that was going to market. She was not producing enough milk for her keep, let alone making any money from her. The hog that was butchered before Thanksgiving was just about gone. It was time to fill the pantry again, with beef. It was in the middle of January on a Sunday morning after the milking and all the chores were done. Mr. Blank, his housekeeper, and her child went to visit a friend for the day.

My father and I were going to lead the cow home a quarter of a mile to butcher her like we had done last year. Tony came out of the barn with the cow, leading her with a halter. I had the barnyard gate open. The cow butted Tony to the ground and started to run to the open gate. I beat the cow and closed the gate. I asked Tony as he was getting up. "Are you all right?"

He said, "Yes"; then I asked, "Where is the rope? Did it break?"

He said, "I took it off."

I said "That was bright." I was surprised at myself for saying something like that! I never talked to any adult that way, let alone my father.

Tony was walking slowly toward the cow. Tony was about six feet from the cow and she charged, butting Tony again and knocking him to the ground. I said, "Let's open the barn door and let her go to her stall and we will start over."

Tony said, "OK."

As I opened the barn door, Tony was not on his feet yet and the cow was coming after him again and rolled him over again. Tony hollered, "Shoot the SOB before she kills me!"

The temperature was around sixteen degrees at that time of day. In the early morning it was near zero. It was cold. From Christmas to the end of February the normal temperature during the day is around eighteen degrees for a high and around zero to five degrees below zero through the night. I was sweating and nervous as hell. I grabbed the barrel of the .22—my hand froze to the gun barrel. The cow wouldn't go back into the barn. She was looking at Tony on his knees. I was about fifty feet away, aiming my gun at the cow now, and I said to Tony, who was between me and the cow, "Where in the hell do I shoot her?"

"In the eye so she can't see me."

I was trying to shoot the cow in the eye; the cow kept moving her head up and down. Tony was hollering, "Shoot! Shoot!" over and over. The cow looked like she was going to charge. I shot; the cow stopped moving her head, just standing there.

I had only one bullet in the gun. I had a couple more bullets in my pocket. I put one more in the gun while Tony was hollering, "You missed! Shoot again."

This time I shot the cow in the eye. I could see the blood coming out of the eye. I put another bullet in the gun.

Tony said, "Don't shoot anymore. Get the rope."

I brought the rope. The cow hadn't moved; blood was running down her face. Tony tugged on the rope. The cow took one step and fell to the ground. We examined the head. The first shot was in the left eye! The cow was not dead; she was unconscious. Our butchering tools were home. Tony went into Mr. Blank's house to get a knife to cut the cow's throat. Tony was mad. He wanted to save the blood. Now he had to get a horse out to pull the cow to a big tree in Mr. Blank's yard so the cow could be butchered. I went home and got the knives, pails, and pots we needed. When I got back with Mike and Tony, Jr., helping me with the stuff, Tony had the cow hung in the tree. The horse was put away. Mike and Tony, Jr., washed the blood away with water from the watering trough in the barnyard. Tony butchered the cow; we put parts in the pails and pots and some in an empty feed sack. He cut off a piece of beef for dinner; we carried what we could carry home and had a Sunday dinner. The rest of the cow Tony would move to our house on Monday.

After dinner we relaxed by the wood stove; the heat from it felt good. We were just about to go to sleep when Tony said, "Let's go to work."

I said, "I'll see you later."

Tony said, "I'm going to need help tonight." Tony was sore all over and bruised here and there. The four of us went to work that night. Mr. Blank wanted to know what happened, and he was told.

12

There Was Always a Price on Pleasure

After supper when there was snow on the ground two or three times a week we kids and a few of the adults in the area would go sleigh-riding in the moonlight. There were a few hills in the area that were over a mile long. We would meet on the one that was considered best and sleigh-ride until midnight. One night as I was going down the hill on my sled, three more kids, clowning around, piled on top of me, halfway down the hill the runners of the sled cut through the crust in the snow, the sled got buried in the snow, and we all slid off the sled, me on the bottom. When we stopped at the bottom of the hill there was blood in the snow. The right side of my face was hurting; the skin was worn off, the flesh showing through. One woman with us took me to her home and bathed my face with egg whites. Between the egg whites and tit balm salve, in a couple of weeks you would never know how bad it was.

One night in February, Tony came home from work without his lantern and says to me, "Henry, get the twenty-two and go halfway back toward the barn. There is a raccoon in an oak tree."

"Which one?" I said.

"I left the lantern at the base of the tree. It won't come down as long as there is a light at the base of the tree."

I walked back to the tree; there is no moon. It is black. Everywhere I look it is dark. I could see silhouettes of the trees and fence posts. Then I saw the lantern. I got to the tree; it took a while before I could see the raccoon. As I moved to shoot at it, the raccoon would move to the other side of the tree. We did this a few times. Finally, I picked up a stone and threw it to the other side of the tree and wait for the raccoon to come to my side. It did. It was about forty feet up, coming through the crotch in the tree—made a perfect target. I shot at the raccoon; it did not fall. I don't know if I missed it or it died caught in the crotch. I was trying to see. I was going around the tree with the lantern trying to reflect light on the raccoon; the lantern was no help. The raccoon was too far up the tree to get a pole that long. I guess I'd have to climb up. I had climbed trees that high before, but not at night and I was cold. All of a sudden the raccoon fell to the ground. I pointed the gun at it just in case. It was dead. After dinner Tony cleaned it for tomorrow's supper and I had another fur.

Mom was in a world of her own. While I still lived at home Maggie never got up for breakfast with us kids. Mom always made supper and did a minimal amount of housework. One day Mike, Tony, Jr., and I came home from somewhere to do our chores. Lina is in the backyard crying; a chicken was on the ground by the chopping block, tied up with string, its legs chopped off. Mom wanted a chicken for supper, and we boys weren't home to kill it. Maggie told Lina to kill a chicken. Lina could not hold the chicken with one hand and swing the ax in the other hand. Lina needed both hands to raise the ax so she tied the chicken up. When she placed it on the chopping block the chicken would not holds its head still. Lisa missed it a couple of times. Just as we came home

Lina cut its feet off and started to cry. Well, big brother to the rescue (not the chicken's).

In May, in addition to doing our regular chores, it was time to start planting, digging in the garden. The doctor started to come up for the weekends, and he had odd jobs for us to do.

Just before school was out Tony said he thought it would be good for me to work for another farmer rather than work for Mr. Blank this summer. I said OK.

Mike and Tony, Jr., took over doing all the chores around the house. I told the doctor that my brothers would work for him in my place. I also went to a few other farmers I would do odd jobs for, telling them that Mike and Tony, Jr. would be available.

13

About Law and Justice

The weekend that school was out the farmer I was to work for came to the house on Sunday. He and Tony visited awhile. I got a few bits of clothing I had. We said good-bye to everyone. We went about ten miles to a town called Wallkill. This man was a justice of the peace for the town of Wallkill, New York. He also owned and worked a 360-acre farm and had about seventy head of cattle, forty-five milking cows. The judge had a wife who also helped with the milking, morning and night. He had another hired hand named Charley.

The judge had electricity on his farm; they had milking machines. They had a modern barn; you could drive a wagon and tractor in the barn to clean the stables. I helped with the milking that first night. The judge had a tractor that he used and a team of horses that Charley or I used. The first week I learned the routine and what was to be my responsibility. I was at the judge's side most of the time the first two days. The judge had a retarded brother and a senile uncle living with them. The judge's wife cooked, cleaned house, did all the laundry, and helped with the milking. After I learned the routine, the judge's wife did not help with the milking. She was a pretty woman, who kept herself well groomed and smiled and laughed most of the time. I liked being around her. After being there a few days I offered to help clean the

71

dishes and pans. She said I didn't have to. I said, "I don't mind; I've washed dishes before."

I was living with the judge a couple of weeks. After breakfast on Sunday until milking time was "time off." It was too far to go home and visit. I was working on a puzzle in the living room. There was a knock on the door. The judge was reading the Sunday paper and Mrs. Judge was working in the kitchen. The driveway was 500 feet long, and I could see it all the way out to the road. I could also hear a car go by on the road. I asked if I should get the door. The judge said yes. There were a man and a woman at the door, and they wanted to see the judge. They wanted to get married.

The judge said, "Come in." His wife came out of the kitchen, and the judge said, "Come here, Henry, and sign this paper and be a witness." I was a witness to a wedding once a week, and for a couple of wills, and at many other events. We would be eating supper, when we would leave the table, marry the couple, then go back and finish supper. Supper on the farm was when you would go over the events of the day. A lot of the time you would be in the field by yourself with the horses, cattle, or tractor fixing fences. So the only time you could really talk at length was suppertime. Supper on most days would last over an hour. The judge was on call twenty-four hours a day, seven days a week. We would be in bed and someone would wake us up for the judge to marry them. We would come in for lunch from the fields and a couple would have been waiting all morning for the judge to marry them.

I remember being in a hay field in the middle of July, over ninety degrees. We all stripped to the waist in the heat. We were loading hay onto a wagon. The sheriff, with two men and a boy about my age, drove out in the field where we were working. They were fishing without a license. The judge had a box bolted onto the tractor under the seat. It had a Bible, a ledger, a couple of law-books, and a gavel. We would stand around the back of the tractor, and the judge would hold court in the middle of a hay field. The hired hands were the witnesses. The lawbreakers paid their fines and walked away grumbling.

We were in the barn one night milking, when the sheriff and his deputy came into the barn with a man in handcuffs. He was in a fight. The man he had the fight with was at the doctor's getting stitched up. This first man was charged, and the judge said he would have to spend the night in jail. He threatened to kill the judge. The judge said, "Be careful or I'll send you away for a year."

The man said, "I didn't say anything."

"Henry, what did the man say to me?" the judged asked.

I said, "I'll kill you," to the judge.

The man said, "He is only a kid!"

The judge said, "His eyes and ears are in better condition than yours and mine. He would be a good witness."

The prisoner hung his head and said, "I'll go." He went quietly.

Charley was sick; he did not feel very good on Sunday morning. It was in the middle of August. He said I could use his bike if I wanted to go see my family. He was staying home this weekend. I had not seen them since I left in June, almost eight weeks ago. When I got home about 11:00 A.M., Mike and Tony, Jr., were cutting the grass around the house. Tony was working in the garden, and Mom was inside getting Sunday dinner ready. We always had a big dinner on Sundays. It was the only time we could relax and enjoy the food. All the rest of the week we worked just to survive; whether it be for comfort or food, it was always work.

It was when we were sitting down to eat that I noticed Lina was not there. Mike said, "Lina is living with Mrs. Stern and taking care of her baby for her."

I said, "Mrs. Stern that lives just past the one-room schoolhouse?"

Mike said, "Yes."

I said that she was too old to have a baby. It seems she adopted a child and needed help in caring for the baby. Lina was a kid herself, only eleven years old. Mom said they wanted her because Lina was a good worker. I was happy for her. These people had electricity and steam heat, and the woman cooked. "I'm sure Lina doesn't work any harder than she did here," I said to Mom. (Dr. Boutzell had something to do with Lina going to Mrs. Stern.) Mike and Tony, Jr., had to take up the slack. I said, "Anyway, I'll be home Labor Day weekend to go to school. That's only three weeks away. You guys [meaning Mike and Tony, Jr.] will see Lina every day in school, and she only has to walk about half a mile to school."

I enjoyed the visit with my family. I thought on the way back to the judge's farm that it must be hard on my parents living in these tough conditions. If only the electric company would string the electric wire—the poles were all in the ground now. It's almost a year that they were in the ground.

When I got back to the judge's, the exchange of words, "How is everybody?"

"OK, said to say hello. I said, 'I'll see you when school started.' "

The judge had enough land that he had three large pastures for the cattle. He would rotate their use. This week the cows were on the far end of the farm and had to go a half-mile or better to get to the pasture, through a passageway of fencing on both sides, about twenty-five feet wide. There was no problem putting them in the passageway; the cows would take their time getting to the pasture. When it was milking time they just would not come in by themselves. I had to go get them. It was hot; the cows were in the woods in the shade. I got them moving toward the passageway. All of a sudden a thunder and lightning storm came up just as quick as you could say "storm." It was raining really hard, the wind was blowing, and I could hardly see the cows. With constant thunder and lightning, half of the cows were in the passageway and the rest were coming along just fine. I was maybe one hundred feet from the fence when a bolt of lightning hit the barbed wire fence. The two strands of wire lit up like a lightbulb. It made a deafening noise; the flash ran down the fencing splitting all the fence posts for about five hundred feet, setting some of them on fire. The lightning bolt knocked about twenty cows down, killing seven of them. Where I was standing my hair on my body stood straight out and I had a tingling sensation all over my body. The storm was over in about fifteen minutes. I went straight to the barn and told the judge what had happened. I must have had a funny look on my face, or my hair was still up; I don't know. The judge said, "Go to the house and get cleaned up. You look awful." He said, "We will see who comes in." I had mud and dirt and grass all over me. I don't know if I did it running back to the barn or if the lighting splashed it on me when it hit the ground. The next day the soap factory sent a couple of trucks and hauled the dead animals away.

We had a great hay crop this year. It was the most hay the judge had harvested in years. The barn was full, two large haystacks near the barn. The judge felt very good about the extra hay.

Charley wasn't feeling good at all Labor Day weekend. The doctor thought it best if Charley was in the hospital in Newburgh. The judge asked me to stay until Charley came home. He said, "You could go to school in Wallkill and the Missus will buy you some clothes for school and a new pair of shoes." I started eighth grade in the town of Wallkill in 1941. While Charley was in the hospital I used his bike. I went home and told my family the news that I don't know when I'd be home!

Right off the bat, the coach, seeing me play sports in gym class, wanted me to play on the soccer team, the football team, the basketball team, you name it. I didn't get involved in sports after school—I had to go home and work. I only played sports in gym period in school. Two inside games that were played in school hours were Ping-Pong and badminton. I became champion of both. I beat the coach in badminton. That was a mistake. He just kept hounding me to play after school. The coach kidded me, saying I was a sissy because I would not go out for any contact sports. I said, "I'll play any sport you play in gym period; I'm right in there."

Coach said, "I mean after school, stay and practice."

I said, "Forget it, Coach, I don't think you hear me."

About a week after Halloween, one night we had just finished the supper dishes when a couple of cars came into the driveway. About ten people came to the house. The sheriff was leading the pack. There were five high school boys I had seen in school, three fathers, one lawyer, and the sheriff's deputy. Someone on Halloween night had stolen twelve mailboxes and thrown them into the Wallkill River, while walking across the bridge, you could see them in the bottom of the river. I saw them in the river on the way to school the day after Halloween. I went for my hat and coat to go outside. The judge said, "Henry!" really loud. "Stay here. Get Clair; get Charley out of bed [Charley was home from the hospital but bedridden], and get my brother, Ed. I want all the witnesses I can get." The judge was mad! It is a federal offense to go into someone's mailbox, let alone steal one. Such things as being disrespectful and showing disregard for authority, in those days, were not tolerated. The judge would not take any nonsense. He was tough and went by the book. We grew up with having respect for our elders. You said, "Yes, Ma'am," "No, Ma'am!" and "Ma'am, if you please, whatsoever," and smiled.

The judge wanted to send these young men to jail for six months. The lawyer and the fathers were arguing. "It was a joke; the kids were having fun. That's too harsh a punishment. They will have a police record. These young men have a chance to be officers in the army or navy, but not with a criminal record." This went on, back and forth, for over an hour. We started to get bored with hearing the same thing over and over again. The fathers were willing to buy new mailboxes and have them installed. The judge said, "No good. These boys have been in front of me before. They are not sorry for what they did. It is a joke to them. I'll tell you a way out. These young men will go into the river this Saturday, retrieve the mailboxes, and install them where they took them from." The moaning and glowering! (This was the first week in November.) The judge said, "That's not all. I want these young men in the service by Christmas." The lawyer said, "These men won't graduate from high school until June."

The judge: "If they are in jail they won't graduate either! By Christmas or they are going to jail!" and he slammed the gavel down hard. "Now out of here, all of you." After they were gone, he poured himself a half a glass of whiskey, first time I saw him do that.

I said, "Judge!"

"Henry," he said, "these young men are troublemakers. They have been in front of me a number of times, for a number of charges, from suspected burglary to vandalism and fighting. Henry, don't feel sorry for them."

The war was in the papers and on the radio more and more. The judge listened on the radio about the war in Europe and said it wouldn't be long before we would be in the war, too.

Charley was feeling better now and working all day long now. I said to the judge, "I guess I can go home now."

He said, "If you want to. How about next weekend?"

I said, "Good."

The kids in Wallkill School were teasing me and making all kinds of remarks about me being a traitor, that my relatives are fighting against us in the war. I never did have a friend in Wallkill School. I liked living at the judge's. I worked hard and I was treated very well. I felt like I was part of the family—nice people. I went home the weekend Japan bombed Pearl Harbor (1941). I was thirteen years old then.

When I got home they had electric lights. The power was turned on that week. The electrician wired the house like you would a chicken coop. They ran the wire on the outside of the walls and along the top of the baseboard, across the ceiling to the center of the room. Each room had one light in it and one double plug. The light had a pull string. The only thing I could say about it was, we did not have to fill the kerosene lamps anymore.

I went to New Paltz School the second week in December. When I got on the bus everyone wanted to know

78

where I was or had I finally decided to go back to school? After it was explained to everyone, I realized I had no paperwork to bring to school stating that I was not playing hookey. When I got to school I went to the principal's office. I told him I was working for the judge in Wallkill, I didn't have any records with me from Wallkill School, and I was in the eighth grade. The principal took care of the paperwork. He brought me to one of the three rooms that were for the eighth grade and introduced me to Miss Higgins, a teacher and supervisor, as a new pupil. When I went to seventh grade here the year before I had long hair and I wore jeans, a work shirt, and high work shoes. Now I was wearing slacks and shirt like the other kids and a pair of low shoes. Some of the kids in eighth grade remembered me from seventh grade. By Christmas time I had made friends with most of the kids again.

At this time in eighth grade I was thirteen years old. I had gone to eight different schools over these few years. I had met over five hundred different children in my classes that I attended, and I knew their names. I could see their faces when I daydreamed. Finally, eighth grade through my junior year I finished going to school with the same children in my class.

Grandpa came to visit the Sunday (1941) before Christmas with just two of his sons, Nick and John. They were going into the army. Two of Grandpa's sons had already gone in the service. They brought clothing, a small radio, toaster, some dishes, pots and pans, and a few other kitchen utensils. They were gifts from Uncle Joe! He had lost his wife, who died giving birth; the baby lived. Joe gave these things to his sister. Uncle Joe went into the navy, and his mother-in-law took the baby. Grandma was sick and could not travel. We never knew

Uncle Joe was married; another uncle, Eugene, was married and had about three children then.

As I'd always done (I guess it was a habit I got into while going to the one room-school), I would do my written homework in school. I would do my algebra homework, fold it and put it in my algebra book, and leave it in my desk, as I did with book reports or a science problem, same thing. A couple of weeks after I was back at New Paltz School the supervisor, Miss Higgins, wanted to speak to me about my homework. It seems another kid in algebra and I had the same mistakes on our homework. He accused me of copying his homework. He was failing before I came back to New Paltz. Miss Higgins knew he was copying; she just wanted to know if I was giving him the homework to copy. I had a slight dyslexic problem; no one picked it up in school. Once in a while I would copy a math problem wrong. I would reverse a few of the numbers. I would do the problems, and they would be right. (That's a mystery!) But when you checked just the answers from the correction sheet, the answers were wrong. I told Miss Higgins what I did with my homework. From then on when I got my homework done in school, I had to give it to the supervisor in charge of the subject.

My poorest subject was English. In my junior year they took math away from me. I always scored a 99 percent in math homework—they did not believe in 100 percent in those days. As a matter of fact, every day in math class the teacher had me go to the blackboard. She would give me a problem to write on the blackboard, whether it be algebra, geometry, or trigonometry, and have me solve the problem and try to make me tell the class how I arrived at the answer. I could not explain it clearly to everyone, but the answer was right. My junior year in high school they had me repeat sophomore English and

also take junior English. They tried to make my speech proper. The people I worked for were from Europe. They were all kinds and each one spoke with a different accent. I lived with them and worked for them so I talked like them! (I still can cuss.)

14

I Am American

It was the beginning of March (1942) and I was coming home from school. It was about 4:00 P.M. Trapping season was over, (Thank God!), or I could have had my .22 rifle with me. As I approached the house there was a New York State Police car in front of the house, with two state troopers; big men, over six feet tall. My mother was standing on the front porch. Mike and Tony, Jr. were sitting on the steps crying. When I saw the troopers I wondered what had happened. They had our little radio and our Brownie camera that Uncle Joe gave us in their hands. I said, "They were given to us; we did not steal them." We never stole anything. What we had was given to us by different people. I put my hands up and wanted them back.

One trooper looked at the other, then said, "Son, you are Italian. We are at war with the Italians."

I said, "I'm an American; so are my mother and brothers."

The trooper went on to say, "There is a German family down the road, isn't there?"

I said, "I don't know what they are. As far as I know they are Americans, too. Why are you taking the radio and the camera?"

"Your father could make a shortwave radio out of it."

I said, "He doesn't even know how to plug it into the socket. We only got electricity two months ago. We just

got the radio from Uncle Joe, who is in the Navy right now. We don't even have film for the camera. How are we going to know what happens to the Lone Ranger?"

Mike and Tony Jr., were crying. Mom was saying to me, "Come here, sonny; don't make the troopers mad."

I started to beg for the radio. "You keep the camera," I said, "we have nothing and you want to take the only thing we have that is valuable to us. It's the only pleasure we have. We have nothing; we work hard just to be comfortable. I'm an American. It isn't fair."

The troopers looked at each other. They gave me back the radio and camera. I must have smiled from ear to ear. For the first time they were smiling. They said they would check on us every now and then, so don't fool around with the radio.

They went through the whole country and harassed all the Italians and Germans in the area. Like my father, Tony, they were all taken somewhere and questioned, then returned home. They were given ID cards which they had to have on them at all times. At one point in the inquiry they wanted to send Tony back to Italy because he was a soldier in the Italian army in the First World War.

Farming was an important industry at that time. If they took Tony off the farm, the farmer would have a problem working his farm. All the available young men were being drafted into the service, so Tony stayed where he was.

About a month after the troopers left us, they did come back. Mike, Lina, Tony, Jr., and I just came out of the woods coming back from fishing. We saw the state police car. I dropped the rifle I was carrying. As we came around the back of the house the troopers were coming out of the house. I said, "Is anything wrong?" They said

no. They gave each of us a candy bar and were off. We went inside and Maggie was eating a cookie. They had left a box of goodies on the table.

15

New Friends Down the Road

In 1942 Dr. Boutzell sold his farm and whatever he had in New York City. He bought a house in New Paltz and opened up a practice not far from the school I was going to. The new owner of the farm was a cartoon artist for a paper in New York City. He wanted to get this farm in working order again. He spent a lot of money repairing the barns and finishing the house and buying livestock. With all this going on he gave us things to do, too. We were sad when everything he wanted done was done, no more cash.

Next to this farm, a little farther away, about a half-mile from home, another family from New York City bought a farm about the same time that Dr. Boutzell bought his farm; they knew each other. These people went into chicken farming and were fixing up the house and a big barn. There was an elderly man working the farm by himself. He lived in one room of the house. His son-in-law came from New York City every Friday night and worked all weekend fixing the house. On Sunday night he would go back to New York City.

I went over to the farm one weekend. The man was working on the house with the older man as his helper. As I found out later, he was his father-in-law. The older man was having trouble giving the younger man tools or whatever items the younger man wanted. I started to

give the things to the younger man; he was on a scaffold. I almost put the items in his hands, and fast. I started to read his mind and gave him what he wanted next. In about three or four minutes he said, "Pop, you are feeling better," and looked around and saw me standing next to him. He saw the older man sitting down; he looked bewildered.

The older man said, "Donda! I have to water the chickens and collect the eggs. The boy will help you; won't you, son?"

I said, "Yes."

Well, I found a new place to pass my time. The older man's name was Pfiffer. I called him Pfif (Fef). Donda was the son-in-law. They called each other by their last names. I don't know why! That Sunday evening when Donda went back to NYC the car was loaded with eggs and butter. When Donda came up from the city on Friday night the car was loaded with materials he needed to fix the house.

The farm next to Mr. Blank's, where Tony worked, was sold to Spanish people. They had two boys about Mike and Tony, Jr.'s age. Their oldest boy's name was Inrica, the equivalent of Enrico! My father was happy. Finally, someone moved into the area he could talk to in his language and be understood. My brothers found a needed new friendship with the two boys.

That summer I worked with Donda on weekends and during the week I worked with the old man. I got paid two or three dollars and a candy bar a week. We put new siding on the house, fixed all the windows, and painted all the rooms. Near the end of August the house looked great.

Labor Day weekend Mrs. Donda came up to the farm. She couldn't come to the farm with her husband before

because she had to work. She was a nurse. They wanted to buy another cow or two to make more butter to bring to the city. With the war going on, things like butter, eggs, and fresh meat of any kind were hard to come by in the city. They asked me if I would help Pfif with the work in the morning and evening after school. They would pay me three dollars a week. I said that I would.

When Tony got up in the morning and left for work he would wake me up and I would get ready to go to work, too. Only now I was going to Donda's to help Pfif. I was given a room to change into my work clothes at night after school and in the morning before school. Pfif would make me breakfast. In the evening I went home to eat supper. In the morning I would milk the one cow they had. There were more head of cattle to take care of, too. I took the milk to the pantry at the house, ran the milk through the milk separator, put the skim milk and cream each in a separate container, washed everything, got ready for school, had breakfast, and was on my way to the bus stop by seven o'clock to catch the bus about quarter to eight. The evening there was a little more work. The chickens, about three hundred of them, did their laying during the day. I would water and feed them, take a quick look at the nests and collect the eggs that had been laid after Pfif collected eggs in the afternoon. I had to feed the livestock in the evening, too. I would finish up about the time Tony was finishing his work at Mr. Blank's. I used to get to the driveway of Mr. Blank about the time Tony would be coming up the driveway to the road. We would walk home together for supper.

16

Finally Got to Know Tony (My Father)

The first night I met Tony at the end of the driveway, that night was the first intimate relationship I had with my father. The next year, for fifteen minutes every night, I would ask my father about our family and the past. On occasion on these nightly walks home together with my father I asked him what happened years ago. (I was thirteen years old.) "Why did you go to jail? What was wrong with Mom?" It didn't come easy. Tony would say a funny response and get off the subject. I would ease off and go with the flow, and at that point of our talk we would be in front of the house and we stopped talking. The next night Tony would have an incident that happened that day that was either funny or scary. It took the whole time we walked home to tell the story. I found out weeks later about our family, according to Tony's story. He was good at telling stories. It took just about all winter, fifteen minutes a night walking home with him, to get this information. Tony said that he had gotten into arguments with Maggie (Mom) over everything from housework and cooking to taking care of her children and it just got out of hand. He had guns of all kinds in the house; his brothers-in-law left their guns there at the house, too. They used to come to the farm and hunt often. He and Maggie

fought and Maggie was shot over her eye. Tony was very sorry it happened.

I said, "What did Grandma say?"

Tony said that Grandma and Grandpa wanted to know if he loved Maggie.

I asked, "What is love?"

Tony said, "You have lots of love."

I said, "I do?"

Tony said, "Yes," and that he loved Maggie.

I said, "If it was an accident, why did you go to jail?"

"Because of a law, having an unlicensed handgun."

Grandma and Grandpa never did condemn my father, Tony. From what I noticed from then on and looking back, I believe my grandparents liked my father. I don't know what really happened. I never heard a derogatory remark from my uncles or aunts about my father or mother! Well, we will never know the true answer; everyone who knew it is dead, except the one who really knows! Maggie! She is ninety years old this month of March 6, 2000, at the time I am writing this story. Maggie resides in a senior citizens' home for people with Alzheimer's disease.

I found out my father had gone to school in Italy. School was not compulsory in Italy at that time. In those days families paid for schooling for their children, so only the ones who could afford to send their children to school got an education. Evidently Tony's father could. Tony had an eighth-grade education, supposedly equal to a high school education in the United States.

Tony used to write to his mother often. His handwriting was beautiful, I mean, the letters were perfect, all the same size. If you saw his handwriting you would not believe this writing that I am doing is by his son! I could not read Italian. Every time Tony wrote to his mother he

would send her money. We didn't have a pot to pee in, and he sent his mother money. One of the nights walking home with Tony I asked him, "How come you send Grandma in Italy money when we need things here?" Tony said, "It is worse in Italy with the war." Tony asked why I wanted to know.

I said, "All the money that I earned I gave to you to help us; you bought things for the house from Montgomery Ward's catalog, but we still need more things."

I asked what Tony's father (my grandfather) did for a living. Tony said his father was a medical doctor! I was surprised! Whenever we got hurt or really sick we did not get a doctor. We were lucky that Dr. Boutzell came into our lives. (When Dr. Boutzell moved his practice to New Paltz and before, we never paid him any money. He would not take it from us. Whenever we went to see him he was given a fresh-killed chicken, eggs, or something from the garden, and if there was nothing to bring him we would do some kind of work he needed done around his house.) Tony never talked about his father. I found out after Tony (my father) died that my Grandfather Togna specialized in abortions. In the early 1900s in a Catholic country, he made a lot of money, I was told. That my father sent money to his mother did not make any sense.

Sometimes as we walked home together we were wondering if Mike and Tony, Jr. had done their chores at home, feeding the pig and chickens and collecting the eggs. Sometimes they would forget that they had work to do at home before supper. They would be having so much fun playing with their new friends or undertaking a little job that would take longer to do than they thought.

On those fifteen-minute walks with Tony on the way home for supper, we made plans to cut wood or to butcher

an animal, what to plant in the garden (all the fun things kids my age did), and speculated on what the future would bring and wishes and desires. We developed a one-on-one friendship where my ideas and suggestions were equally weighed with Tony's. Whenever I made a suggestion, if it wasn't too hairbrained or too costly, Tony agreed and I "did it."

17

Boy, Did I Learn a Lesson!

Donda wanted to butcher a steer one weekend and take the meat to New York City. When he went back to the city that Sunday night the car was loaded to the roof with meat, eggs, butter, and chickens. Every weekend Donda went to the city loaded to the roof with farm-fresh food. He would buy a pig from a local farmer, and we would butcher it. I was getting to be a pretty good butcher. Mrs. Donda came to the farm that summer and stayed on the farm; she gave up nursing. We got more chickens and more beef cattle. I was asked to stay at the farm with all the extra work to do. I went home on Sundays to visit my family and have dinner. They gave me a few more dollars' pay, and Donda would bring me a big chocolate Hershey bar when he came up on Friday nights. I would take it home on Sunday and share it with Maggie, Mike, and Tony, Jr. My father would not eat any unless he had the whole bar. A couple of weeks later I talked Maggie, Mike, and Tony, Jr., into giving Tony the whole chocolate bar. He refused to eat it. My father held fast to the theory that he wanted us to believe, whenever there was fruit or sweets or dessert of any kind, unless he had a large amount or a number of the items available he did not care to eat any. Lina believed this for years. Many years later Lina would bring Tony a big bunch of bananas or bring two quarts of ice cream, one for Tony, whenever she came home to visit.

That Sunday night as we loaded the car for Donda's trip to the city, Mrs. Donda said to Mr. Donda in front of me, "I'll bet Henry doesn't have any chocolate left!" I said it was all gone. Donda lectured me all the time when we were loading the car about how I should learn to save some candy for later on and not eat it all at once. Next Friday Donda gave me the Hershey bar and I thanked him. He said "Next Friday you have to show me a piece of the Hershey bar or you don't get another one."

I said, "OK."

That Sunday I went home with the candy as I always did and before I gave it to Maggie I cut one square with the *H* in it, wrapped it up in the candy wrapper, and put it in my pocket. Maggie and my brothers wanted to know what I was doing. I told them if I didn't show Donda a piece of chocolate next Friday, no more chocolate.

The next Friday Donda asked after we unloaded the car, "Have you a piece of chocolate?" I showed him the chocolate I had. Donda said, "I hope you didn't eat it all at once."

I said, "No, I didn't."

In the middle of the following week Mrs. Donda asked me how much of the chocolate I had left. I said, "I have one piece left for Donda."

She said, "That's all, Henry?!" in disgust.

The next Friday I showed Donda the piece of chocolate; I got the new bar.

We are eating supper on Sunday; the car was loaded with food for Donda to go to the city after supper. Mrs. Donda told Mr. Donda that the candy was gone by Wednesday. Mr. Donda said, "Henry!" I said it was gone on Sunday except for the one piece. Donda got up from the table, came over to me, and started to lecture me some more. I said I took the candy home to my mother

and two brothers and only took four pieces for myself. Donda stood there with his mouth wide open, not saying a word.

Mrs. Donda got up laughing, came over, and hugged me, saying, "Henry, we should have known."

Donda said, "I'm sorry, Henry, that I misjudged you."

Next week Donda didn't ask for the piece of chocolate I had; he gave me three of the big Hershey bars. "Henry, if you want to eat them all, go ahead." I said, "Thank you."

18

Plenty of Beef (Could Not Eat It)

Dr. Boutzell had moved out of New York City to New Paltz into a one-family house and hung out his shingle. When school started I would bring eggs, butter, or a chicken to him once a week when I went to school on the bus. While in town I would get the *Daily News* and a magazine for Pfif. Sometimes I was given some kind of medicine by the doctor to give to Mrs. Donda.

I had three cows I was milking at the Dondas'. One of the cows would not get pregnant. Every month we would take her to Mr. Blank's farm to get bred. Her milk was way down, so it was decided she would become beef. Well, we butchered her and found she was in calf, about four months. The Dondas felt bad; she was their first cow and we had two of her offspring in the field. Some of her went into the freezer on the farm and the rest of her to NYC.

That Easter Sunday was going to be a big celebration at the Dondas'. Mrs. Donda's sister Mary, with her two daughters and boyfriend, was coming to visit from NYC. Mr. and Mrs. Boutzell were coming, too. Everyone wanted to see me; we hadn't seen each other for almost a year. I went home just to visit with my family for a few hours. I did not eat anything. I went back to the Dondas' and met everybody; then we went to do my chores and milk the two cows. Some of the visitors helped me, which

made more work, but it was fun for them. Donda rang the supper bell, time to eat. Pfiffer and the Dondas came from Bohemia and they knew how to cook. Mrs. Donda's dumplings were out of this world, and the beef stew, pies, and all the trimmings and goodies she made were great. Everyone was having a good time. Wine was poured for everyone. The main topic was the shortage of fresh food because of the war.

Mrs. Donda served everyone her dumplings and beef stew. Everyone started to eat. I finished my portion and looked up at the big cauldron of stew in the middle of the table. As I dug in for seconds, everyone was watching me eat. No one else was eating; then Mary's two daughters, almost in unison, said, "Henry! How could you eat Bossie?"

I said, "She tastes very good," as I put another scoop of stew in my plate.

Dr. Boutzell caught my eye. We looked at each other for a second; he shook his head, saying, "No."

Mrs. Donda cleared the stew off the table. I helped her in the kitchen. I said, "I'll take this home later."

We had plenty more food to eat, another glass of wine, and the party was in full swing again. The rest of Bossie went to the city.

During the war many families raised a steer or hog and butchered it. That was the only way you could get fresh meat for a period of time. Every once in a while someone asked me to butcher his animal. I would do this on a Sunday for five dollars and some of the animal back for payment. I gave Tony the five dollars and Maggie the meat.

19

Was It a Dirty Trick or Clever?

This one family had a steer. It was big and ready to butcher, only they couldn't see themselves eating the steer they had raised. The man asked me if I could swap his steer with someone else's. I said I would try, understanding his plight. The few people I asked were not interested. On Sunday he would come by and I told him no luck. I told Pfif about the swapping of the steer. The old man said, "Butcher it and give it back and tell him you traded it with someone."

"Who?" I said. "Everyone in the area will know in a week if I did it."

Pfif said, "Have him bring the animal here, and when Donda butchers one you tell him you will change it."

I told the man to bring the steer to Donda's. The next week he stopped by. I said nothing yet. That weekend Donda told us he was not going to bring any more beef to the city. He said next week he was moving his things from NYC to the farm and would start to work in Poughkeepsie, New York for IBM, doing government work.

The days were getting longer now, that Friday after school Pfif and I butchered the steer and got rid of the hide and head. The weather was still cold. I cut a piece of meat off each hindquarter for myself. He did not want any organ meats. Pfif took the meat to the house; Mrs. Donda was pleased. When the man came Sunday I told

him his steer went to the city last week. He gave me ten dollars and a front quarter of the steer and made a comment about this steer not being as big as his. I said it was the best I could do. He left the farm saying he was not going through this again with his family: "We will do without."

Mrs. Donda thought what we did was terrible. I teased her. I said, "What makes you think that Bossie went to the city?"

20

Newkirk and Taking Stock of Myself

Arthur Newkirk had stopped by the house asking if I would work for him this summer after school was let out. I went to see him, and we worked out a deal for one dollar a day, room and board. I started to work for Mr. Newkirk around the middle of June 1944. I was fifteen years old.

Most of the abandoned farms in the area were being worked by young men around twenty-four to thirty-four years old. If you were running a farm or bought one, that was better yet; you would not be drafted for military service.

Mr. Turner was farming next to Arthur Newkirk's. I was working with Art mending the fence between the farms. Mr. Turner was helping fix the fence, too. I was at Newkirk's a couple of days, and Mr. Newkirk was bragging to Mr. Turner about me, saying that I was a good worker. Mr. Turner asked me didn't I have a brother at home.

I said, "Yes."

"Do you think he would work for me this summer?"

I said, "I think so. I'll ask him."

After work that night I went home and asked Mike if he wanted to work this summer. He said, "Yes." We told Tony what we planned. Tony, Jr., would be home with Maggie to do the chores around the house. Tony,

Jr., was eleven on the twenty-fourth of June. He was now in charge. He could do the work any way he wanted to. Tony, Jr., didn't like it at all; now he had to answer and explain why things were not done. Tony wasn't sure Tony, Jr., could handle it. I said I was younger than him when I had to learn what to do on my own. He had it all laid out for him.

It was time to take account of the situation. Maggie, Tony, and Tony, Jr., were home, Lina was at Mrs. Stern's, Mike was at Mr. Turner's, and I was at Newkirk's, and Helen, whom I hadn't seen since she was about four months old in August of 1935, was living with people by the name of White. She was about nine years old now. None of us had seen her or talked about her. We were so busy just working to stay warm and getting food and trying to be comfortable that Helen never came to mind. I did not know it then, but Helen did not know we existed—better terminology (we did just exist): Helen thought Mrs. White was her real mother.

When I started to work for Mr. Newkirk I told him to keep my money; I didn't want it now. I wanted to buy Christmas gifts for my family this year. I didn't go anywhere to spend the money until after I got my bicycle.

That summer Tony got a telegram saying that Grandma had died. Maggie was the only one who went to the wake and burial. Donda took Maggie to Mahopac for the funeral. Maggie stayed two weeks at Grandpa's. Tony, Jr., was at home alone with his namesake, Tony, Sr., and had to do everything. Now he got a taste of being responsible. He always would slide out of many things, being the youngest. He let Mike and me know about it when we came home on Sunday. We said, "Join the club." Tony, Jr., was always bitter and felt sorry for himself. He was a pouter all the time. Tony, Jr., was not a happy

kid. I began to understand why. I couldn't help him; that was the way it was. He would not accept it. It was tough living in those days.

During the first summer I went to work for Newkirk, we had a violent storm, wind, rain, and hail. It ruined a lot of crops and damaged a lot of buildings. It blew one of Mr. Newkirk's silos down; what a mess. It's funny how people react to things. The storm ruined so much of the corn we planted, we only harvested enough to fill one silo that fall. Mr. Newkirk said, "See, Henry? God knew what he was doing." Arthur never went to church, and that was the first time I heard him say "God."

I loved harvest season. The month of October all the farmers got together and went from one farm to another for three or four days at a time to fill the silos with corn ensilage. The women would also go to the farm where the silo was being filled and cook for the men. The women outdid themselves in the kitchen. Everyone worked so hard and the laughter was loud all day long. If something broke or a wagon got stuck in the mud, these men went to the task of fixing what went wrong with such ease and such a positive and confident attitude you would not think anything was wrong. The corn kept coming to the silo until it was full. After the day's work the problem was talked about with a comical air and more laughter. Nothing fazed these people; whatever happened was taken in stride. At that time of the year in the farm country the farm boys were able to take time off from school.

I had the Montgomery Ward catalog open after work every night for about a week the first week in December. What I wanted to buy for my family would cost about $150. From July to December, for five months, by saving $30 a month, I had the $150 to order my presents. I bought everyone a coat, hat, gloves, and boots, which we

never had. At Christmastime Mr. Newkirk took me home on Christmas morning with the presents in his truck. After I gave everyone their gifts a few remarks like, "Wow!" or, "I sure can use this," did not come forth.

Mike was looking at me. I guess he saw the bewildered look on my face. Mike's remark was, "Why did you get us gifts?"

"I wanted to make everybody happy," I said. No one said, "Thank you," and no one else had a gift for anyone, and that was that. "Merry Christmas." We never gave one another presents before that Christmas, and our father never got us any gifts for Christmas either, never! In my whole life! I don't remember anyone getting a gift from my mother or father. They were preoccupied with themselves. They had no self-esteem. I don't know where the hell they were.

Winter (1944–45) was very cold and there was a lot of snow. When I walked home on Sunday through the woods hunting, it was hard. I managed to shoot something for the table for my parents.

Hank's father, circa 1932

Hank, four years old (1933)

Hank, seventeen years old, just before going to bootcamp (1946).

Mike, Hank, Tony Jr.,
December, 1946

Left to Right: (back)
Warner, Hank (front),
Huff

Newfoundland, 1947

Lina visiting Mom and Pop in the summer of 1947.

(left to right) Jenings, Lt. Anderson, Karass, Cook, McCallister, Pocheco, Sulinski

Training Submarine, New-
foundland

Mountains nicknamed Mae
West, Newfoundland

Nautical exercises, New-
foundland

Big guns, and landing ramp

Packing marines like sardines.

Wet suits in Newfoundland

Hank (standing), Clemensen, White (back row) Day, ?

Stern of the USS *Carpellotti*

Bow of the USS *Carpellotti*

Hank Togna in the Parthenon,
Athens, Greece, 1948

Abdul Mukis Bin Jilur, 1948

Cook, Warner, DiMartino, Persian Gulf, 1948

Togna, 1948

Chief Boone (medic) swabbing our ears to prevent fungus, January, 1949.

A good day of fishing.

North Chesapeake Bay, 1949

Chief Perry

Hank and Lina, 1949, first time exchanging
gifts.

Maggie with Frances, Bette's parents, Mary and Mack, at Hank and Bette's wedding. November 16, 1952

Bette, Elisa, Hank Jr., Frances, and Hank, January 6, 1957

Elisa (seven years old), with Hank Jr. (five years old) in front of the new house in Randolph

Christmas Day, 1973, Hank, Bette, Frances,
(front) Elisa and Hank Jr.

(left to right) Frances, Hank Jr., and Elisa, 1996

(left to right) Nick (grandson), Bette,
Joe Jr. (grandson)

Hank, October 1999

Hank loading a deer on the Blazer, December 1999.

21

Flood Advance
(Training for UDT?)

After a hard winter, in March of 1945 the weather turned warm, suddenly a lot of rain. The rivers started to rise, breaking the ice that was frozen completely across the rivers. The ice was over twelve inches thick. The ice broke into pieces about four feet by eight feet on the average, and floated downriver to near where the Shawangunk Kill and Wallkill River met, just a few hundred feet before the bridge. An ice jam formed in front of the bridge; the ice and rising water threatened the bridge. The road was closed, and the water was flooding all the farms back of the ice jam. Mr. Newkirk realized that the farmer nearest the jam, Orsback, did not know what would happen when ice formed a dam at the bridge. We were coming back from town and Mr. Newkirk went to the farmer and told him he had better move his cows out of the barn. He had a friend with an empty barn he could bring them to. The farmer was farming this land about four years, and every spring thaw water would flood over half of his farmland. He knew that. Mr. Newkirk said, "Yes, but, when there is an ice jam like now, right here where we are standing the water will be eight to ten feet deep." We were standing between the house and the barn. Mr. Newkirk said to him, "About every six or seven years this happens." The farmer did not take Art's warning serious.

The next morning Spence, on the other side of the Shawangunk Kill from Art's farm, called Art and wanted to know if Art could spare me for the day. The farmer down by the ice jam had about four feet of water in his barn. The cows were in the barn with their heads tied up to the ceiling to keep from drowning. Now they thought the water was going to go over the cows' heads and needed help getting them out.

Art said, "Damn it! I should have let the cows out of the barn yesterday," and explained to Spence that he had stopped by and told the farmer what to expect.

Spence said, "Well, he needs help now."

Spence had a couple of riding horses; so did a few other farmers. The farm was about four miles downriver from Art's and Spence's farms; the river separated their farms. On an average day you could not see the river; today it looked like a lake. It had flooded half of Art's and Spence's lowlands, and all the farms along the river were flooded. About eight farmers gathered by the road alongside the river. The water was just covering the road. A half-mile down the road it was two feet. The men walking with their hip boots had to slow down. I was on one of Spencer's horses with three other men, four all together. By the time we got close to the barn we went through four-foot-deep water. The horses started to get spooked and frightened as we rode them into the deep water. The water was "only" three feet at the barn. Orsback said "We have to hurry; the water is rising an inch every five minutes."

I slipped off the horse into the cold water. I gave my horse to an older man to hold. Two other young men and I went into the barn. What a sight to believe. Orsback and his hired hand had tied all the cows' heads up to the ceiling so they would not drown. The water was halfway

up their bodies. We were given a knife to cut the rope; we didn't have time to untie them. The ceiling was getting closer. The water was very cold. I was so excited and moving as fast as I could. I think I was actually sweating—how could I tell? I was wet all over. I didn't feel cold then.

It took a while to get all the cows out of the barn. There was not much more than two feet of airspace to the ceiling when we got the last cow out. The water was so deep now that the smaller animals had to swim. The man who had my horse was off the horse, standing on something holding him. I said, "You take him up the road, which has over three feet of water running over it. I'll help to get the herd started to high ground; then I'll follow you out." He was afraid of the horse. He would take his chances by himself.

I got on the horse. The man said, "Take my jacket." I changed jackets; it felt good. It must have shown because he smiled back at me and said, "Now help get these cows out of here."

We started to drive the cows to high ground. The water was quite swift. The animals had trouble going the way we wanted them to go; some got into the current and were gone. The horse I was on almost got caught in it. I whipped him with the end of the reins. He responded well. We drove the cows in water six to eight deep across two large fields to high ground, almost a half-mile. The cows did not know it, but they were swimming over fences that ordinarily held them in that field. The evidence that we crossed over the fences was apparent when we got to high ground. It was clear a number of cows had their tits cut off by the barbed-wire fences we swam over. We got the cows onto the road. Heading to the barn, Art told Orsback about yesterday. We men on horses went back

to see if more help was needed. Some city kid (he was older than me) about eighteen, whose parents had bought an old farm not far from here, had just gotten his driving license, and went speeding past a group of us who had just gotten to the road after looking for stragglers. About ten minutes later, as we went up the road to catch up with the herd, we saw ahead of us a cow down in the road and the car in the field with a few cows. This kid hit and killed a cow, hurt a couple more, and was hurt himself. It was just past the one-room schoolhouse. Spence said to me, "Henry, it's time to go home." We turned onto schoolhouse road and headed home. Now I was starting to get cold. I started to shiver. Spence said, "Let's walk the horses." We got off the horses and started to run, leading the horses for a while, then got back on until we got to Newkirk's farm.

Mrs. Newkirk had coffee on and Art got out a bottle of whiskey and I had my first shot of whiskey and my second shot and my third shot of whiskey. (I had had wine at Grandpa's many times.) Art said, "Change your clothes, Henry!" I felt warm and said they would dry in a little while. Spence left for home leading the other horse that I had ridden. Art and I started to do the chores and get ready to milk. In the interim I told him all that had happened that day.

The next day Art came home that afternoon with all the dope. Mr. Orsback had lost ten cows, including the one hit by the car, twenty injured so badly they were sent to the market. All his chickens, pigs, sheep, goats, and the like were gone. Mr. Orsback was the only farmer who lost livestock. The other farmers' land got flooded over, and some had land damage. Later that day the state highway department successfully dynamited the ice jam after two tries.

That summer after school was out another young farmer trying to stay out of the army asked me if my younger brother would work for him. Tony, Jr., went to work for his room and board with the young farmer. Tony, Sr., did not get a pig anymore and the chickens got to be fewer, so he could handle the chores when he came home from his work.

Late in the summer of 1945, after Japan surrendered, the material for the new silo came. We did our regular work milking, plowing, planting, mowing, and putting hay in the barn. Mr. Newkirk hired a carpenter to build the silo. In between doing all the other work we would help the carpenter. Sometimes we would spend all day with him or a couple of hours, whatever was needed. By the middle of September we had the silo built, forty feet high by eighteen feet across, with no roof. After the silo was filled with silage, in October the carpenter came back and I helped him to build the roof on top of the silo. The carpenter wanted to hire me. I told him I was joining the navy next year. He tried his damnedest to get me to work for him.

In June 1946 a friend from school and I went to Poughkeepsie to join the navy. We were both seventeen years old. Our parents had to sign for us, giving consent. Ace signed for me, and I signed for Ace. Our parents knew.

22

Epilogue

Everything I have written about my life and the people that I came in contact with is true. The names (other than my family) are similar. There are a lot more incidents that happened. I just wanted to explain to my family that I walked over three miles to school and it was uphill "both ways." Not only that; it rained or snowed each way, too. Ha! I just wanted to give highlights of some of the events and point out how tough my young life was. It was tough! I always contributed to my (our) family needs. When I think back, I remember I was always happy. I enjoyed going out and finding something to do. In my wandering and exploring while afoot, whoever I came upon, I always said "hello" to them. If they needed help, I helped them and went on my way. I still do! I like people. I have always enjoyed being alive, and I am glad that I was born. If I had to live my life over again, I wouldn't mind if I had to live it the same way. Every day it got better.

My brothers have different childhood memories than I do, even though we were raised in the same home and are the product of the same parents. I realized that times were hard in our childhood, but I always thought things were pretty good and relatively normal under the conditions which we lived. While the others would see it as a dark dismal experience lived out in a horrible place they

did not like. We all have selective memories of our past. I choose to see and think of all the happy moments and to hell with the negative ones. Things turn out best for people who make the best of the way things turn out.

Once a week every Saturday a breadman came to our house around 4 P.M. My father gave me $1.00 to give the driver, we kids unloaded the truck of stale bread—twenty to thirty loaves of hard Italian bread. It was all gone by the next Saturday.

Another incident—it's no wonder that I am alive. During Christmas vacation, 1940, from school, Mr. Blank's housekeeper and her son came over to ask us to go sleigh-riding on this nice Saturday afternoon. It was cold and the snow was hard; it would be good sleigh-riding. I said, "No, we can't go! We have to cut firewood first." Dot said she would help us. We were sawing and splitting the logs in our cellar. Dot was sawing wood with Mike on the two-man saw. I was sawing a log with the smaller two-man say, halfway through the log. I was sawing (I am not paying attention) and cut halfway through my thumb on my left hand, about a half-inch from the tip, through my fingernail and all. I bled like a stuck pig. We got a feed sack and cut it into strips two inches wide. I was wrapping my thumb, trying to stop the bleeding. I lost a lot of blood, so much I wanted to sleep. I finally stopped the bleeding. Dot wanted to know if they could go sleigh-riding now. I said, "I don't care what you do; I'm going to sleep." I curled up on the floor in back of the stove. I was cold. I put my jacket on and went to sleep. Neither my mother nor this woman, Dot (about twenty-four years old), was concerned or alarmed about the way I was behaving or the fact that I had lost a lot of blood. Dot wanted to go sleigh-riding because there would be other single males there on the hill. We kids were her

camouflage. Maggie was in her world getting things ready to make supper. I slept for two days! Tony came home late and left early in the morning. He thought I was just tired. No stitches, no antidote of any kind. After I woke up I had something to eat and I resumed my duties. No one bothered me while I was asleep; they just let me be. I kept bumping my thumb and it would bleed a little. It took a long time to heal. I don't know how or why I never got an infection working around cow shit, trapping and skinning wild game. Mystery?

Mr. Peterson did not own the chicken farm. He rented the farm. He was a carpenter by trade and got a good offer by the federal government somewhere out-of-state. That was why he sold out. The war made work for a lot of tradesmen.

Dr. Boutzell, Mr. Donda, and Mr. Pfiffer were friends in New York City before they came to the country to live. I think the war had something to do with Dr. Boutzell's move to New Paltz. Mr. Stern was an administrator of a hospital in New York City. That's why I think Dr. Boutzell had something to do with Lina going to work for Mrs. Stern. They did a wonderful job making a decent life for her.

Mr. Stevens had cancer; it was too much for him to fight. He did hang himself in that big oak. I missed him.

While I was in the navy Mr. Black had a nervous breakdown. He had to be admitted to a hospital. His family sold his cattle and shut the farm down. My father and Maggie moved, and Tony went to work for another farmer in the area. I found this out when I came home on leave for Christmas in 1947. No one was in the house; everything was gone. I had to ask a neighbor what happened and where my parents had moved to.

A picture with the four of us children, left to right Tony, Jr., Mike, Lina, and me, showed what we had to wear in 1938, 1939, and 1940. We went to the one-room schoolhouse dressed in such rags; nothing fit us. Everything was given to us. Where we lived hardly anybody would see us. We were in the fields or barn most of the time. September, 1940, when we started school; for the first time we got new clothes that fit (denim work clothes). We changed out of them into our rags to work, the electric pole in the back of Mike in the picture stood by itself for over two years before it got more company and wire. The workmen went through and put the poles in the ground that they could dig deep enough not using dynamite. Later they came back and finished the other holes with dynamite. That took a long time.

I don't know if you noticed that most of the time I did what I wanted to. I never asked if it would be all right. I always took care of my chores and would work the other deals that I made after I took care of my obligations at home.

Dot, the housekeeper for Mr. Blank, went back home with her son. He was about fifteen at the time. Dot had to leave home and high school in the early thirties because she was pregnant. Tough living for everyone in those days.

Tony and Maggie lived by themselves now with just a dog, no other animals, electric refrigerator and freezer, and oil heat. My parents started to live a more comfortable life.

Lina died in 1956 at twenty-six years of age in childbirth.

Mike died in 1958 at twenty-six years of age with Hodgkin's disease.

127

Tony is alive, living in the next town a few miles north of me in New York. And Hank is still kicking as of May 2000.

The home I went to live in 1933 was the home of Max Rosenbloom, a light heavyweight boxer who held the title from 1930 to 1934, the man with me in the boat and the eel.

Part II

1945–50, My Navy Years

23

Enjoyed Boot Camp

This period in my life is my life from high school to my discharge from the navy. In high school I was an average student. I had to do my homework in school during study periods. I could not take homework home because I had work to do. From fall until spring about an hour after supper we went to bed. Four o'clock in the morning came around quickly. I never stayed after school. Another reason was because I lived fifteen miles away and there were no buses or trains to get home. During basketball season this year, a few guys who played on the teams were hurt and the coach was begging me to stay and play. I told him I had to go home and work. This Friday we were going to play Wallkill School, our rival. He said, "I'll take you home tonight after school and talk to your father." On the way home to Mr. Newkirk's, I told him I lived with these people and worked for my room and board. Only a few kids in school knew this. Fifteen miles and about thirty-five minutes later we pulled into Mr. Newkirk's driveway. I took Coach Campbell to the barn where Mr. Newkirk was working. I introduced them and went to the house and changed from my school clothes to my work clothes. I came out to the barn. Mr. Newkirk and Mr. Campbell were talking. I went to work doing my chores and getting ready to milk the cows. I was milking and Art and Mr. Campbell were still talking. About a half hour later Mr. Campbell said good night to me and left.

About another half hour later, as I was coming out of the milk house and Art was going in, he said to me, "What was this all about?"

I said, "Didn't Mr. Campbell ask you if I could have Friday off from work to play basketball?"

Art said, "No. We talked about you; that's all." Art was a tease, so I figured I'd wait my time and he would tell me what was said.

We finished our work and went in the house for supper as usual, and nothing was said. I figured when Art wanted to he would tell me. We went to bed, got up at 4:00 A.M. and did our work, and nothing was said that morning. I rode my bike to meet the bus and went to school. It was 10:00 A.M. before I found Mr. Campbell. I asked him what happened.

He said, "I started to talk to Arthur and he thought you were in some kind of trouble at school and he thought I was there to find out what kind of a boy you were at home. After a few minutes he understood there was no problem at school and I wanted you to play sports at school. He said I would have to speak to your father. So I left it at that."

I said, "Well, what?" Mr. Campbell said, "Henry, you go home and work. I had no idea what you had to do. I thought you were giving me a lot of bullshit. I'll find another way to beat Wallkill." We lost the game with Wallkill.

During my junior year the subject of college was brought up often by Mr. Campbell and my friends in school and this business was going on in Congress about making service at least mandatory for every single male who was eighteen years old or after he finished high school. I had decided to join the navy when I finished my junior year. Why wait one more year? So in June 1946,

132

one friend from school was in the same circumstances that I was in. We agreed that after the Fourth of July we would join the navy. We had to go to Poughkeepsie, New York, to register, about thirty miles away. The chief petty officer at the U.S. Post Office in Poughkeepsie filled out all the papers, and we had to report to New York City at a given address (which I don't remember) in time to get a physical and go to boot camp. I guess it was the sixteenth of July that we got to New York City for our physical. While we were being examined a doctor took me to one side and asked me where I lived and what I did after school and weekends. I told him I worked on a farm. Then he asked me if I drank raw milk, milk that wasn't pasteurized. I said yes, at least two to three quarts a day. He said, "Well, you have a few black spots on your lungs; it is nothing." Whenever I went for an X-ray, the doctor said, I should tell them that. I was raised on raw milk. I didn't have TB, but because I drank raw milk the bug was in my lungs, but dormant. I passed my physical; my friend did not pass his. He felt really bad; he left and went home.

Later that afternoon, on the sixteenth of July 1946, a couple of hundred young men were sworn into the navy. Then they said we could go home for two weeks and report back there on the first of August 1946. They gave everyone a slip of paper with his names and a reporting date on it. Everyone left but me. The recruiter asked me what was wrong. I told him, "I left home early this morning; I said good-bye to my family and friends." I had three dollars, my toothbrush, and toothpaste as I was directed by the recruiter in Poughkeepsie. I was not going home. At that point I wondered what happened to Ace, my friend who didn't pass the physical. That's all he had on him, three dollars, a toothbrush, and toothpaste. A little

while later the recruiter gave me a slip of paper to stay at a YMCA overnight with breakfast in the morning and report back here by 8:00 A.M. the next day.

They put me on a navy bus; it made a few more stops in NYC, picking up a few more young men and some navy personnel, then headed for the state of Maryland. Of course, I didn't know that then. Everything was a secret. We made a few more stops, I'm not sure where. I think it was Philadelphia, Pennsylvania, and Baltimore, Maryland, and then on to Bambridge, Maryland, our destination. We pulled up to a big area with an eight-foot-high fence with barbed wire on top and marine guards at the gate. I felt like I was going to a concentration camp, like the one they threatened to put my father in during the war because he was Italian. The bus pulled up next to a large building. They hustled us out of the bus into the building. Inside there looked to be three to four hundred men in various stages of undress. We were each given a cardboard box and told to undress, put all our clothes and shoes and socks, everything but our toothbrush, toothpaste, and wallets in the box, put our home address on the box, and give the box to the man in the window marked: POST OFFICE. Then we were each given a slip of paper with what clothing we were to have and how many. Then we got in line to receive our new clothes.

As we came to each window, bedding, pants, shirts, underwear, shoes—the clerks behind the window were throwing the clothes at us, two of this, four of that, six of this, and whatever. You were asked what size you were, and the clerks would give you any size. When you started to argue with them, they would say, "Exchange with someone with your size." Well, at that point I was at the underwear window. The clerk threw a size-40-waist underwear to me. I'm not a stupid kid, but I am naive

and I argued with the clerk. A chief petty officer came over and wanted to know why I was holding up the line. I told him, "The Clerk gave me a size-forty-inch waist. There isn't a man in this room that's a size-forty-inch waist. You are the fattest one in here, and you don't wear a size forty." The chief told the clerk to give me my size. I said, "Thirty-inch waist." Thirty-two was the best they could do. They were out of thirty-inch, so he says: "Well, the word went on down the line and everything I got was a size thirty-two inch."

As you got your clothes you would stuff them in your mattress cover to carry everything that was yours. When you got to the end you were to dress in the blue jeans. As you went out the door someone called a number to you. As you went farther on in the heat (it was July 17, 1946, in the state of Maryland; it was hot) you were directed to a group of men. When the group numbered 120, a couple of petty officers instructed us to pick up our gear and follow them. Well, I had no problem picking up my mattress cover full with my clothes. It was not as heavy as a 100-pound sack of feed, which I was used to. As we followed them, over half of the young men could not pick up their mattress cover, so they dragged them in the dirt. We walked over a third of a mile to our barracks at the end of an area that looked like a barren ten-acre field with barracks all around it, about 150 feet apart. (The number 126 popped into my mind as I was writing this. I think it was the number of the barracks we would be staying in.) There were a lot of the barracks around what looked to be like a ten-acre field, and we soon learned its name, the grinder. The barracks were two stories high, with another 120 men on the second floor. The buildings were about 50 feet wide and every bit of 200 feet long.

There was a dormitory area that had sixty double-decker-type bunk beds, thirty on each side, and a shower area with toilets at one end of the building, an office and two more rooms separating the dormitory and the toilet area. In the middle area was where our petty officers in charge lived. The area at Bambridge was gigantic. There were about ten more grinders one after another, plus a huge area for our training just as big.

We were up and to muster by 6:00 A.M. on the grinder; then we marched to the mess hall. Everything we did, to eat, to different schools, to exercise, to the canteen, whatever we did we did it together. The only time we were on our own was on Sunday. The barracks were dirty and dusty, paint peeling all over the place. We were told if we cleaned the barracks and made things neat we would get the whole weekend off to go into town. We did not know it at the time, but the town was an intersection with a general store, a red light, and a few other buildings and small businesses here and there. The rest of the area was hay fields or woods.

This was on a Thursday of the second week. Boot camp was six weeks during the war and I was in the last class that went to boot camp for six weeks, and I believe that September they started to close Bambridge down. Those guys who were given two weeks' leave and went home to NYC, well, I heard when they came back, starting the first week of August, boot camp was extended to twelve weeks and they were sending everyone from the East Coast to the Great Lakes for boot camp. Anyway, we worked our butts off cleaning and painting Thursday and Friday. Saturday at 0800 hours we stood at attention in our whites and our polished shoes, waiting for the captain or whoever was to come. This man showed up with brass all over his hat and jacket looking like a doorman

at a fancy hotel, stopped by the door, made a big deal out of putting a pair of white gloves on, stood there a few seconds, reached up over his head, ran his white glove along the top of the door jamb, brought his hand down . . . it was black. He said no weekend off. We were to be punished for being so careless, and he left. He didn't even come into the barracks. The chief said to us, "Out of your dress whites and into your working blues and be on the grinder in twenty minutes."

The distance around the grinder was about one mile. It had twenty barracks on each side and about five on each end. The chief in charge said to everyone, "Five laps around, running, no walking." We started to trot around the grinder; everyone was doing fine the first three times around. Remember, it was in July, around the twenty-fifth of the month. The men started to fall to the ground from the heat. Three or four days before, we all had been inoculated for ten or twelve diseases, and three or four of the men were still in sick bay. By the fifth time around there were maybe six of us still running. This event was duck soup for me. Another fellow and I were running side by side after the third time around. As we had about one thousand feet to go, he said to me, "Let's pour it on from here to the barracks," and he stepped up the pace; he was about twenty feet ahead of me. I was saying to myself. *This fellow wants to be number one.* So I upped the pace and passed him, saying, "Come on, slowpoke." I get to the barracks steps a few seconds before him. Now he wanted to know how many trophies I had, what my fastest race was, whom I had raced against. When I told him this was my first race and probably my best time, he said, 'You are a private person, aren't you?"

Within an hour the ones who could helped the others to the barracks. Getting a chair and examining the door-jamb, we found that black shoe polish was smeared on the jamb. Some fellows got sore. I thought it was funny. The six weeks at boot camp went by fast for me, with fire fighting, shooting, rope or semaphore, drilling on the grinder. With it all, I gained thirty pounds in six weeks. My clothes fit me now like they were tailored for me. I think I was the only one who gained weight.

The first of September we graduated from boot camp. I went home on leave for two weeks. When I left home for boot camp I weighed 150 pounds. Six weeks later after boot camp, I weighed 180 pounds. I held that weight until I retired; now I weigh 190 pounds. When I got home everyone I met thought the navy was a great institution. After all, in six weeks they took a kid and made a man out of him. They fed me well; I ate all my meals and more. When I asked for another spoon of food as we went through the chow line, every now and then the cook would be there. He would say, "If you throw any food out in the garbage you will be punished." I would say, "Punish me." I would get another spoon of food. Boot camp was a vacation for me.

Around September 14 I reported back to Bambridge, Maryland, at a distribution center nowhere near our barracks, and I didn't see anyone I had gone through boot camp with. I picked up my gear and got on a bus with many other sailors; the next morning we arrived at Little Creek, Virginia, for the first time. We stayed in a barracks similar to the one we had in boot camp. Each day a number of names were called from a holding area that we reported to each day. The second day everyone was called into groups of thirty, forty, or fifty men and sent to a ship either at the Norfolk naval station or here at

Little Creek. Everyone but me. The chief petty officer in charge asked me my name.

I said, "Togna" (tone-ya).

He looked up and down his list of names and finally said, "Tog-na."

I said, "It's 'tone-ya.' " He said, "I have a wise guy here."

I said, "I'm not a wise guy; that's the way you pronounce it."

He said, "From now on, it's Tog-na."

My real name is Enrico Togna. When I was a kid, everyone but the teachers called me Henry, even my father. The teachers called me Enrico because I signed everything "Enrico." Now, for the next three and a half years I was going to be called Togna. In those days we did not use first names in the service.

I don't know what ship I would have been assigned to had I heard my name called earlier. The next morning I was loaded into a small boat and ferried to an APA, *New Kent,* a troop transport at anchor in the Chesapeake Bay off Little Creek. I was assigned to the first division. The ship was understaffed. We had a chief petty officer named Childress and a third-class coxswain named Hart and four other seamen who were in for about a year. A few days later we got four more men. They put us to chipping paint on the landing craft, then painting everything with primer. Well, this tub of a ship was not what I dreamed of being in the navy. I didn't think the navy had ships like this. I thought they were all battleships, destroyers, and cruisers. A couple of days of chipping and painting, while I was chipping the paint I would chip cursewords and then chip them out. At the end of the third day at 1600 hundred hours the whistle blew to knock off for the day. I was about to sit down and eat my

supper when Chief Perry came in and started yelling at me. I was chipping paint on a landing boat that was stacked three high. At the end of the day he went up to see how I was doing. When the chief looked down in the bow of the landing craft, in the middle of the ramp, from side to side, about six feet across and about two feet high were the words: FUCK YOU.

I said, "Just as soon as I finish my supper I'll go up and chip it out."

He knocked my tray of food to the deck. "As soon as you clean this up, you get your ass up there and chip that whole ramp tonight before you go to sleep."

While I was chipping away a couple of sailors strung an extension cord for lights, plugged in a radio, sat on the gunwale of the boat, and chitchatted. It was taps by the time I got done, 2200 hours.

Well, I fixed myself with the chief. Every shit detail that came up was mine. As a matter of fact, I would just step forward and Chief Perry would say, "Get it done, Togna." We learned to run all the winches topside. We would go to sea and cruise around for six to ten days, then come back to port. We never tied up to a pier; we anchored in a channel or bay or harbor. We anchored in what was called Hampton Roads off Norfolk because of a storm. It lasted three days. The second day of the storm, the captain of the ship, who was a full captain by rank, still could not get dockside. He wanted to go ashore and called for Hart, our coxswain, and his running mate. The first division was also in charge of the captain's boat, or gig, as it was called. Well, the boat tender told Hart he didn't want to go with him; it was too rough out there. Chief Perry asked me if I would go. I said, "OK." They lowered the gig with the captain, Hart, and me in it. We had one hell of a time getting unhooked from the hooks

140

of the davit. The waves were four to five feet, and the wind was blowing us around to make matters worse. Finally, we were free and on our own headed to shore. We pulled into the landing. How Hart found it I don't know. It was 1800 hours and raining lights all over the place. The captain said he wants to be picked up around 2400 hours.

Hart said, "I'm not going back to the ship."

Captain asked, "Where will you be?"

Hart said, "The usual place."

We tied up the gig; the captain was gone. Hart and I went to a bar. Hart was drinking beer, I was drinking soda. We played darts and shuffleboard all night. Around midnight the captain came into the tavern. He was under the influence of alcohol. Hart was feeling no pain. Each had a few more drinks and were talking about going back to the ship. The captain wanted to know if Hart was all right and capable of bringing the gig back to the ship. Well, you know the reasoning of two drunks. They agreed that they could handle it. It's still raining; the wind was still blowing. We went to the pier where the gig was tied up. The MPs on watch said, we couldn't go out in this weather. Boy, was I glad to hear that.

The captain told the MP he was the captain of the *New Kent* and he had orders to get under way at 0800 hours. Hart started the engine. I cast off the lines and jumped into the gig. Hart was steering the gig recklessly; the captain told me to take the wheel. I told him I didn't know how to handle the gig. He says it's no different from the LCPs (landing craft personnel boats). He had Hart give me a few instructions. It was about 0200 hours, dark as hell, and raining. There were six or seven ships anchored out there, and I didn't know which one was ours. I headed for the lights of the middle ship. When we got

close, what looked like the middle ship was the first ship. Ours was the second ship. I had to bring the gig up to the gangway so the captain could get off. I made two passes; the waves were still about four feet. The captain said, "Come up to the gangway fast," then, just as I am going to hit the ship, "Put it in reverse and gun the engines." The captain was now on the bow of the gig. Coxswain Hart was useless at this point; he was being knocked around the gig like a rubber ball. I had the window on the gig open so I could see. I ran up to the gangway like the captain said, and just as we were going to hit, I put the engine in reverse. I bumped the gangway lightly; the captain was on the gangway, and I don't know if he jumped or I knocked him off the gig, but he got up on his feet and gave me the high sign. After trying to bring his gig to the davit a couple of times, we went back to the gangway, and after a few more tries, a few more men, a little more work, we tied the gig to the gangway. The time was now 0400 hours. My first lesson as a coxswain. We had to carry Hart up the gangway; he was out.

I woke up at 1000 hours; the ship was under way. I hurried to topside. The captain's gig was secured in the davit and the gangway was up. I found Chief Perry; he said, "You decided to join the rest of the world?" I thanked him for letting me get some shut-eye. The crew in the first division had everything under control. Around noontime Perry sent me to get Hart, our coxswain. He was down in the brig; I wondered what happened. I found my way down to the brig, and Hart had all his personal gear in with him. I didn't know where he stayed before. I woke him up and told him Perry wanted to see him. I was on this ship only four weeks at this point. Well, I started with the questions; I'd give just the answers. He was in the brig so many times that Perry decided that he'd move

142

his gear in lock, stock, and barrel, and when he was to be confined they would lock the door after a while. That meant someone would have to go down and let him out. He was such a good inmate, he had the key. When he was to be locked up, he would lock himself in. The captain liked him. Hart was a veteran of the Second World War and had seen and been in action; I don't know where. Hart was also wounded. At one time he was a Second-Class coxswain; at the present he was a Third-Class petty officer. From the night before, I was his mate whenever the captain wanted the gig.

We pulled into Moorehead City, North Carolina, three or four days after some drills out at sea, to see if things worked the way they were supposed to. One day we had target shooting with our .50-caliber machine guns. They were the heaviest guns aboard this type of ship. The target in the air was towed by an airplane with a long cable. The target on the water was a barge with a big white sheet of canvas. All the exercises went well; everyone remembered their lessons. The first division worked well together.

Now, Moorehead City. . . . We pulled up to a dock for the first time. The place was like a beehive, activity everywhere. Within the hour we were the main feature. We rigged our ship to start taking supplies aboard. There were four thousand marines coming aboard plus many jeeps, trucks, half-tracks, all kinds of equipment, and food. If you could get a picture from above, it would look like an anthill with hundreds of men bringing something aboard. Our Chief Perry was working what they call a yard and stay, loading heavy equipment in the hole, which was a large opening in the front deck of the ship that went through all the decks to the bottom of the ship. They also had one at the aft deck that was manned by

the third division. The second division took care of the middle of the ship.

After a couple of hours Chief Perry called me and started to teach me how to run the hoist and swing the equipment through all this apparatus to fill the decks below. As each deck got filled, a cover was fitted over the deck below and we started to fill the next deck up. We had to keep loading the ship. It had to be loaded in twenty-four hours. When it was full, it had to go out of the harbor at high tide or we set for twenty-four hours for the next high tide. In this case, we left in twenty-four hours because there was another ship coming in to take this berth. The chief and I worked the yard and stayed until we had everything aboard. Every couple of hours we would relieve each other for a break, a snack, and a snooze.

At one point as we were loading there were ten pallets with ten coffins that I swung aboard. I asked Perry, "Why the coffins? We're not going to war."

He said, "Togna, there are a lot of accidents in any operation of this size, involving thousands of men. Some die."

We were loaded from top to bottom and over four thousand marines. We were ready at high tide. The kitchen was cooking around-the-clock. They staggered the men in to eat at different times. I was sent to the bakery to help, plus taking care of my regular duties. About half of the marines were seasick; the stench below-decks was terrible.

About five days later we anchored off the Vieques and Culebra and started to unload the marines. We had large cargo nets that were laid over the side of the ship to the water. Our landing craft was lowered into the water and pulled up alongside of the ship, and the marines

scrambled aboard with their gear and rifles. When the boat was filled, the landing craft would pull away and take the marines onto the beach and unload, then go back to their ship and do it over and over until the marines were all ashore. Well, after a number of boats were in the water and loaded and on their way to shore, there still were a few boats on the davits that could be used, only there weren't enough coxswains for them. Hart told Chief Perry I would make a good coxswain. Perry said, "Togna, Warner, Huff, get in that boat." I said that I'd never driven one of these. He said, "It's the same as the captain's gig." They lowered the boat with the two other seamen (just as green as I was) into the water. I was thinking about those caskets I loaded aboard ship. I hoped I didn't go back to Norfolk in one.

I came around to the net with no problem. The sea was calm. We made several trips, then the chief wanted me on deck to run the yard and stay. That was my second lesson as a coxswain. We loaded some gear into the small boats that were on deck. (The gear was on deck.) I was thinking about all that stuff in the hole; we would be here for days unloading. Then off in the distance I saw an LST coming. About an hour later it was tied up alongside another one tied up aft. We worked right through the night to unload. We stayed anchored where we were for a few days. We took it easy for a couple of days, that is, after we cleaned the ship from top to bottom.

We started to cruise through the islands on maneuvers. It was my turn to be helmsman. I was steering the ship in the wheelhouse; other men were doing whatever they were supposed to be doing. The ensign on duty came into the wheelhouse from out on the bridge and gave me a command, eighty-five degrees to starboard, and as I was turning the ship this island about ten times the size

of the ship was dead ahead. I was going straight for the island. About that time the captain ran into the wheelhouse and shouldered me from the wheel and knocked me over to the deck. He was yelling, "Full astern!," turning the wheel like a madman. I was still on the deck, a little dazed. The captain gave the wheel over to another sailor, giving him some instructions. He turned to me, "Togna, you all right?" and asked what my last command from the ensign was. I told him. By that time the ensign was in the wheelhouse. The captain talked with him a few minutes and sent him to his quarters and called for another officer to come on duty. The captain, realizing who I was, asked me again if I was all right. He said, "I didn't mean to hit you that hard, but it was the quickest way not to run aground." When my turn came around again for me to man the wheel, I was there and so was the ensign. To this day I don't know if I fouled up or the ensign gave me the wrong instructions.

We cruised around the Caribbean and Atlantic Ocean heading for the equator. We stopped in Trinidad for a few days' liberty, then headed back to Norfolk, Virginia. We had a lot of work to do on the landing boats, repairing and replacing broken parts and doing the old standby, chipping and painting all over again. When we got back to Norfolk we tied up dockside for the second time, because they had to work on the yard and stay equipment. One time in Moorehead City while loading, I lost a jeep. Just as I got it over the hole to lower it, the brakes on the winch failed and the jeep fell to the bottom of the hole. The four wheels popped off. Thank God no one was under it.

It was the first week in December 1946 that we tied up at Norfolk. We did our daily work routine for the month the ship was tied up at the pier. I went home on

leave for the Christmas and New Year holidays. When I came back, the first week in January 1947, the ship was anchored in the channel again.

In December 1946, while home on leave, I was with my friend Ace Barton. He was the lad who went to New York City with me when we went to join the navy and got rejected. It was cold; there was about two feet of snow on the ground in New Paltz where we lived. Coming back home from being out on the town from Newburgh, a neighboring town, we ran out of gas. It was 2:00 A.M., a couple of miles out of town. Ace was always making one car out of three junk cars. Of course, with this one, the gas gauge didn't work. We walked back to town with an empty gas can and a wrench. It was cold, about five degrees above zero. We came to a street that had many cars parked on it. Ace crawled under one and loosened the plug at the bottom of the tank. The idea was to fill our can, then put the plug back. Well, he dropped the plug into the empty can. He couldn't stop the gas coming out to retrieve the plug. We filled the gas can and let the rest spill onto the road. When we got back to the car we were frozen. We got the car started and I said to Ace, "Let's go back and put the plug back in the car."

He said, "No, we will get caught."

"We have to go back and give the guy the plug back," I said.

On the way back, we saw a police car. I put the plug with a five-dollar bill under the windshield wiper. After this every time Ace came to pick me up to go somewhere, I would make him pull into the first gas station we came to and fill up.

A few days after I got back from leave in January 1947, the ship got under way heading for the Caribbean. On the way down, we fueled at sea. I asked Chief Perry

why we didn't fuel at port. He said, "We have to practice to do these things." A couple of days after the fueling, a hospital ship showed up. We went through the same procedure as with the fueling, except instead of the fuel hose being sent between the ships on a cable connected to both ships, we were going to send a man on a stretcher to the hospital ship. Just before we were going to put the stretcher on a pulley to be hauled away, the cable between the ships snapped. So we started all over again. Now I don't know who the sailor was or if he was the same one who was going in the first place. The ships were side by side about one hundred feet apart, going at least ten knots. The cable this time was slack between the ships; it was so slack the man on the stretcher, when he went to the hospital ship, got dunked twice.

We pulled into Guantánamo Bay, Cuba, and anchored. We had a few days' liberty at the naval base, with a couple of beer parties while the marines were loaded on board, just the men and their equipment. Then we set sail for Norfolk. We arrived off of Virginia, Chesapeake Bay, off Little Creek, and we anchored. There were about a dozen more ships in the area. We had a landing party with the landing craft again. I was assigned one of the landing craft and made a few trips into the beach at Little Creek. Third lesson as a coxswain. We moved into Hampton Roads and anchored near Norfolk Naval Base. This was about the middle of February 1947.

A newsletter was posted on the bulletin board asking for men to volunteer for underwater demolition. I filled out the forms. Chief Perry would not sign them. I asked the ensign I was on duty with when we had the watch. He said he couldn't help me. A couple of weeks went by and I could not get anyone to help me get transferred. It was the beginning of March 1947. The ship was getting

ready for another trip. I decided to go to the captain on our next run to the pier to bring him to shore with Hart as coxswain. I told the captain what I wanted. He said, "If that's what you want, son, I'll sign the papers." I had to have a physical first by the doctor.

While I was in sick bay getting checked out, the chief came in to talk to the doctor and asked the doctor to fail me. The chief did not know I was in another room and could hear him talking. He told the doctor, "I can't lose him. He is my whole division. Find something wrong with him."

The doctor said to the chief, "Don't worry. You'll miss him on this trip only. From what I hear ninety percent of the men fail or drop out of the course and get sent back to the ship they came from."

The chief left and the doctor asked me, "Did you hear that?"

I said, "Yes."

"The chief likes you."

"I know, I like him, too, but I don't like this ship."

The doctor tried to talk me out of going. "Why do you want to go to UDT? Do you know that they swim in ice-cold water with a stick of dynamite stuck up their ass just to blow up a bridge?"

I said to him that I liked to swim and was used to cold water. I would carry the dynamite between my teeth.

He shook his head and said, "You have about four hours before the ship sails, so get going."

As I said before, we did not have running water in our house. We had a pump outside about fifty feet from the house. We got water from the well winter and summer and had an outhouse in the back of the house, a two-holer, as they called them, kerosene lamps for light, and a wood stove for heat, using wood we had to cut by ax or

with a two-man saw. Our school bus would pick us up about two miles from the Shawangunk Kill. It was a river that flowed into the Wallkill River, by a one-room schoolhouse. That was the end of the school bus run; it would turn around and double back those two miles and continue back across the bridge over the Shawangunk Kill and continue its trip bringing the children home from school. If it was a warm day in March, I would tell the kids on the bus I'm going swimming today. They knew when I was going swimming because I would get off the bus at the bridge. Most of the kids thought I was crazy. When the bus came back across the bridge, I would be in the water. I didn't stay in long; the water was cold. I washed myself, and I had to hurry home or to where I worked to earn my keep. Well, living in those conditions, we didn't bathe much in the winter, so when spring came most of the boys would start swimming early. Around St. Patrick's Day, March 17, when we had a nice sunny day we would go swimming. We would bring a bar of soap. At the end of the workday we would swim all summer until Halloween, the end of October. So with the swimming, running, and shooting as a kid, I put a lot of wild game on the table for supper. This doctor had me sized up wrong. As for the mud and the noise from the exploding TNT, that was all that was missing. Of course, I didn't know that then, but I was already halfway through UDT training. As I finish writing this, I just realized I never thought about the APA *New Kent* 217, and over the years on all the maneuvers we were on and in and out of Norfolk Harbor. I never saw that ship again. I wonder if she went to the West Coast or if she got decommissioned.

I'm on my way to Little Creek for UDT. It was sometime in March 1947. I had no idea what I was in for. I wanted off that ship.

24

UDT Training Was Duck Soup

When I got to Little Creek from Norfolk Naval Base by the way of a bus, it let me off in front of a Quonset hut. It had a sign in front with UDT 2-4 on it. I was standing in the road in front of the building and this second-class petty officer said, "What do you want, sailor?"

"I'm looking for Underwater Demolition," I said.

"This is it. You're not supposed to be here until the first of April."

I said, "My ship was leaving on a cruise and I got sent early."

"You must be a real fuck-up!"

"That I am!" I said. I had my papers with me.

He said, "Wait here," and took them inside the Quonset hut.

A few minutes later he came out and took me across the street to the barracks, the same barracks that I stayed in when I came to Little Creek the first time, when I got assigned to my ship. The more I tried to get a change, the more everything kept coming up the same.

Both of the floors in the barracks were empty. Petty Officer Bailey took me upstairs. He said, "There isn't anyone here. Team Four is away, and Team Two has a dozen or so men in it, and they are off somewhere to school. It is just you and me." He was in a little room near the bathrooms that had two double-decker bunks in it. I was

to stay in the dormitory area near the bathrooms so he wouldn't have to walk too far to get me. I settled in, made my bed, put my clothes in the locker, and got into my working blues. The first man I met in UDT was Sam Bailey, with his wonderful disposition. Never changed. A real happy-go-lucky guy? A few minutes later Bailey came into the dormitory. He says, "That won't do. Come with me." We went to the warehouse next to the Quonset hut, where he gave me two pair of pants and shirts, a cap, a pair of swim trunks, and a pair of work shoes. The clothing was green, with UDT on it. "You wear these clothes from now on." He told me to wash up and we would go to chow.

The mess hall was a five-minute walk and there was a line to get in, about eighty men long. We went right up to the head of the line, got our trays, and got served. We sat down to eat, and Bailey said that UDTs don't have to wait in line and we could go up and get seconds if we wanted to, the whole menu, not just one item.

Next morning I got up early from habit and cleaned up, and I was sitting on my bunk waiting. Bailey came out of his room in his shorts to wake me up. He said, "I don't go to breakfast. Do you want a coffee?"

I said, "I've got a coffeepot in my room." OK, I'm off to breakfast by myself.

The next two weeks I was the only enlisted UDT man on base. I ate alone and slept alone. Bailey kept me busy during the day getting the stockroom in order. We had a load of clothing to put in proper bins.

I came back from breakfast and found Bailey in the Quonset hut. There were three men there. One sitting at a desk was Lieutenant Commander Fane; the other two were in their shorts, bullshitting with each other. These two guys liked themselves so much that each time they

walked by the window they would admire themselves and comb their hair, with their reflection in the glass. They finally left. Bailey had me doing janitor's work: "Clean up the barracks, bottom floor, too." A couple of days later I'm in the Quonset hut cleaning and these two conceited asses were there.

They said to Bailey (I don't know their names and never did find out; I don't know their rank, either), "Is this a new trainee?"

Bailey said, "Yeah."

"Let him run with us for a while. He can finish that when he gets back."

Bailey said, "He has to start sometime."

These characters said, "Follow us."

We started to run around the base, up one street and down another. We were running about fifteen minutes, and I was right behind them. We ran a little while longer and then back to the Quonset hut.

Bailey was there with a grin on his face. "Well? How did he do?"

One of the men said, "He will be around awhile."

For the next two weeks, each morning I would run with the conceited ones. After a few days, in the afternoon I would run with them to the beach at Little Creek and go with them for a swim. I stayed with them wherever they went. They didn't talk much to me, only words like, "Follow us," or "Come here," or "Go fetch," commands you would give a dog.

Lieutenant Commander Fane was in his office every day and didn't say much. His desk was piled with papers two feet high.

Around the first of April a couple more men arrived for UDT. Bailey said, "Togna, get these men settled." I became an orderly. I took them to the barracks, next to

get them clothes, then explained the routine. As more men came, I appointed a couple of the first men who came to assist me. By the end of the week we had the top floor full, 120 men, and a half a dozen or so were put downstairs. Bailey said by the time Team Four got back twenty or thirty of these guys would be gone.

While the recruits were coming in, three more second-class petty officers who were in Team Two came back from some school they were away to. They bunked in with Bailey. One of the petty officers' name was Winters. They took over and started giving instructions on what was expected of us and what we were going to do. At any time during our training if we felt we did not want to be in underwater demolition we could drop out . . . anytime . . . pack our seabags and go back to our ship or station where we came from. It was at this point that I realized I was not in UDT and this was where UDT was headquartered at Little Creek. I was kind of depressed! I thought you went to UDT and they would teach you everything you needed to know.

The weather started to get a little warmer, so after breakfast we were told to change into our swim trunks and muster on the driveway between the Quonset hut and the warehouse where all the supplies are kept. The driveway went to the brig for the base in back of our building.

We started by running around the base. They had a small grinder at Little Creek. We would end up there doing physical exercises, or PT. Whatever you want to call it, it was work.

A couple of days after we started training, one morning the Bobbsey Twins, who usually were either in swim trunks or green fatigues all the time, were outside by the Quonset hut in full dress and for the first time I could see

that they were ensigns. I asked Bailey what was going on. Bailey said, "Big secret." That was the response you always got whenever either they did not know or it was none of your business. I never saw the twins again.

At that time it was very confusing trying to know who had finished UDT training or who had to go through UDT training again. Most of the men in UDT Two and Four went through training again either as our instructors with the new recruits or because there was nothing for them to do and they were not going to be sent to a school because their enlistments were ending and only a few had signed over for another hitch in the navy. So when these men left, the recruits, myself included, thought these men dropped out. At any given time four or five men would drop out; two or three of them were from UDT Four and their enlistments were up and they left to be discharged. UDT Four arrived a week after we started our training with the few old-timers from Team Two, Bailey and his three buddies. None of us had seen Team Four before, so we did not know who was who; we all dressed alike.

The first class of UDT trainees was supposed to be replacements for Team Two. Team Four when it arrived at Little Creek had fifty or more men in it. Team Two had fewer than a dozen men in it. Our records were never recorded into UDT files. They were still in the manila envelopes while we were going through training; they were never opened. When you dropped out of training, they just gave you your papers back and sent you back to where you came from. I often wondered if anyone just up and quit the navy at that time. While you were going through training you were not in UDT, or the navy; you were in a manila envelope on a Quonset hut floor. We did not get any pay while we were in training; we were told

we didn't need the pay. We did not leave the base while in training. I'm referring to the first training class.

The first few weeks they ran us around the base on the roads to get us in shape and also to give Team Four time to map out a course for us to go through, in the swamps and sand dunes at Little Creek. By the end of the first week about a dozen men quit. When talk got around that this physical stuff was forever in UDT and next week we would go to the beach and work out and swim, that did it! The other half of Team Four were getting some sort of obstacle course ready for us. They used the natural terrain at Little Creek, the sand dunes, the dozens of earth bunkers that were built to house explosives; some were quite big and high. It made a good running course. The swamps all over the place and the swampy area by the sewage disposal plant were ideal, for what? I don't know what for! But our instructors thought it was a good place to turn men off, and they did. When we ran the tour the first time about twenty men quit. The second time a few days later was when Mr. Richardson, an ensign, got blown out of the mud and water. Men were leaving every day and yet there seemed to be just as many men in training. Like I said before, if there wasn't any work or other duties for the UDT Four men to do, they just came along for the exercise. As the new men dropped out, some of the UDT Four men who were arranging the obstacle course had nothing to do, so they fell right in there with us. A week or so went by and one of these men dropped out. At that time we did not know that his enlistment was up and he left to be discharged. We were thinking this guy was doing so well, why did he drop out?

Around the second week talk was about the hell week. This was where we separated the men from the boys, or was it the boys from the men?

The beginning of the third week, hell week started, with constant harassment, verbal and physical, all week. We would be awakened at 0200 hours to go hiking. At first it was around the base; then we would go to the main gate. Outside of the fence and around Little Creek was a paved road that went parallel with the fence. The rest of the area was dirt roads and swamps, cornfields, hay fields, and woods, and every now and then a shack with black people living in it. Every night at different times we were marched to the main gate and had to run on one of these dirt roads about five miles out into the swamps, harassed all the way, then turn around and come back to the barracks. During the day we ran the obstacle course on base where they would set off a number of blocks of TNT and shower us with sand so we did not eat that day. As time went on we learned to eat in spite of the sand. The instructors would bring us back to the barracks at different times during the day or night and say, "Get cleaned up." After we were cleaned and sitting around, mostly lying down, in the instructors would come hollering, "Up and at 'em!" and we were off to more punishment. This kept going on for seven days. They let us get about four hours' sleep a day.

During this hell week a lot of men dropped out and a few of us who said to one another we would not quit no matter what got to be buddies. Hell week was behind us now, and the verbal harassment stopped, too. I don't know if that was the intent or if the men who were doing the verbal bit left and got discharged.

After hell week the second floor had maybe thirty men left, all recruits, and the first floor had about twenty men left from UDT Four. A lot more men opted to be discharged than Fane thought. The dropout rate of the trainees was a lot more than they expected, too. They

sent out another bulletin for more volunteers for UDT, class to start the first of July.

We went back to the daily workouts, the running, PT, swimming, rubber boat handling, hand-to-hand fighting.

A few mornings after hell week we were awakened at about 0200 hours to get dressed and be ready for a forced march and told anyone who did not make breakfast after the march was out. We were taken to the main gate. We had to run about seven miles out into the swamp on the dirt road and no goofing off. The ones who did not complete the run failed . . . no walking. We started to run and Cain, a little fellow, maybe 140 pounds had sore feet and he begged Clemensen and me to help him run. Cain wanted us to drag him with us. We said, "Come on, Cain; we want to finish, too."

At that time one of the instructors named Winters said, "No excuses, you guys. If you drag him and can't finish, you are out, too."

Clemensen and I looked at each other; we did not say a word. We grabbed Cain and we each put one of his arms over our shoulders and started to run. Cain had tears in his eyes, his feet were sore and bleeding, and every once in a while there was Winters reminding us, "No walking." We pulled Cain with us the whole fifteen miles, and I believe I saw a little grin on Winters's face when we came back through the main gate with Cain between us.

Things seemed to be getting easier now, or we were getting used to this routine. We practiced cast and recovery, that's being dropped off a moving boat into the water (cast) and then being picked up in the water while the boat is running in the water (recovery). All of our classes in explosives, timers, fuses, detonators, and reconnaissance, or whatever we had to learn were verbal. There

were no papers, pamphlets, or diagrams to look at or read. To tell you the truth, I'm not sure that all the men in UDT could read in those days. There wasn't a written test given to us to see what we learned or retained after training. Then, enlisted men were expendable, like a box of TNT or a case of .50-caliber bullets, and we were treated as such. The point I want to make is, everything was done out in the field, so to say, using the real stuff, being shown physically by the instructors, and then you would do it. I will say two things: Everyone listened. The whole time I was in UDT, no one got hurt learning how to do things. And the second thing, our instructors trusted us. These classes were not held indoors. They were on the beach, in the sand dunes, in the water, on the rubber boats, anytime we would take a break from PT or swimming. Everything we learned was one mind-stuffing deal. You had a lot to remember, and we all learned well. We continued doing this stuff over and over until the end of May.

The first of June we were taken about one mile out to sea and had to swim to shore. We were told the men who made it to shore would get their swim fins that we kept hearing about. If anyone got in trouble the boat would pick him up. There were about a dozen of us left by that time. Only one man had a little trouble making it to shore. The boat came over to him. He had a cramp in his leg. Finally it was worked out and he made it to shore, too. We all got our fins that day. One of the instructors said, "Now you guys are UDT men." There was no ceremony, no diploma, not even a letter posted on the bulletin board. We stood out there on the beach at Little Creek in your swim trunks holding our swim fins for the first time with the instructors shaking our hands, saying, "Welcome to UDT Four."

Nothing changed. We got up the next morning and started the same routine. Now we had our fins to practice swimming with. Day after day the running and PT were every morning. In the afternoons sometimes there were classes on everything we needed to know pertaining to swimming apparatus, explosives, boats, karate, jujitsu, reconnaissance, deep sea diving, submarine training, blowing up beach obstacles, and a few more things I can't think of right now.

I want to stress a point about graduation from a trainee to UDT. Fane did not get the men he wanted. Too many dropped out, and too many got discharged. The first class was to be split between Team Two and Team Four. The second class was needed for Team Four. Fane, with a dozen men, was going to promote UDT to the top brass in the navy, and Team Four was going on all the maneuvers, whenever the navy had one. So Team Four now with the six new enlisted men and Ensign Jones and Ensign Richardson had about thirty men. Team Two with five enlisted, including me, and Captain Dunning had about a dozen men. This is about the end of June 1947.

There were about ninety new trainees who bunked half downstairs and the other half upstairs. Their class was to start the first of July. There were rumors going around the whole three years I was in UDT that the navy was going to decommission UDT. So as we went on with our training classes, after we completed a lesson, for what purpose were we doing this if they were going to scrap UDT? I would not get into the discussion. I wanted to learn all I could and I enjoyed the classes, but this rumbling would surface every couple of months.

Mr. Richardson's parents had given him a new convertible as a present for graduation into UDT in 1947. I don't know the make of the car. I was not into cars yet.

The Fourth of July weekend, Richardson and Jones went out and partied. I guess all night. I came back from breakfast on Sunday that weekend of the Fourth; it was about 0800 hours. I looked out the window; across the street was the UDT building. In the driveway with the new car were Richardson and Jones, the top down, a hose in Richardson's hand and a brush in Jones's hand. They were washing out the inside of the brand-new car. They were feeling no pain and laughing, having what looked like a good time. I went down to investigate. The stink was terrible. They vomited all over the car, front and back seats. They removed everything that could be moved out of the car. They were there all morning cleaning the car.

I was in Team Two for about a month; how did I get to Team Four? During our training I became friendly with two other men. Broome, from Texas, he came from a family with money, at least more than most. He had a year of college, and that's all he talked about. The other was Uter; he came from a farm in Pennsylvania. I'm not sure if he finished high school. Uter and I became really friendly, buddies. We had a lot in common, both of us having been born and raised on a farm. Broome was very jealous of our comradeship; he would do things or say things to promote discord between us to the point of trying to get us to fight each other. We were about the same size and weight. We looked alike; we could pass for brothers. Broome finally got under Uter's skin and Uter challenged me to a fistfight. I refused to fight Uter. I said, "If we fight, whoever wins or even if it is a tie, the friendship won't be the same."

Earlier that Saturday we had agreed to go out on liberty that afternoon. Broome had only two dollars, and Uter had three dollars. I had a twenty-dollar bill. I said

I would treat. I had just finished my laundry at this time. I ignored Uter and said, "I'll get cleaned up and we will go out." After I came out of the shower and was getting dressed in my whites, as we called them then, Broome asked to see my twenty dollars. My wallet was under my pillow when I went to the shower. I said, "Don't worry; I've got it." Broome kept on insisting that I show him the twenty dollars. Now! I got a funny feeling in my stomach. I reached for my wallet; the twenty dollars was gone.

I said, "OK, now you have had your fun." I proceeded to finish dressing.

Broome said, "Where are you going?"

"Out with you guys. After all, I said I would share the twenty with you, so who cares who holds the twenty?"

Broome said, "We only have five dollars between us. Where and what will the three of us do with five dollars?"

Now I was looking to Uter, saying, "OK, the joke is gone far enough, you guys."

Now Uter acted, or was, insulted thinking that I was accusing him of taking my twenty dollars. He threatened to knock my block off, and he was not kidding. Broome was standing there with a big smile on his face. He had what he wanted all along. I was so angry at this point, I left the top floor and went across the street to cool off. An officer and an enlisted man were on duty there during the day and just an enlisted man at night. We all took turns standing watch. I went into the Quonset hut, and guess who the officer was Lieutenant Commander Fane.

I told him I wanted to put Broome and Uter on report for stealing twenty dollars from me. He said he wouldn't do it and thought it was just a joke they are playing. Then he lectured me, told me I had to grow up and start acting like a man and start taking care of things myself. He said, "You have to resolve this yourself. Quit running

to Mommy every time something happens." I went back upstairs to Team Two and started packing my gear. Broome wanted to know what happened.

I said, "Lieutenant Commander Fane is sending me to Team Four," and I moved to Team 4.

Everyone wanted to know what was going on. I just said, "I want to be in Team Four." This was about the middle of July, right before a mock invasion on Little Creek was planned with UDT, including a bunch of marines, the whole nine yards.

Monday morning I went over to Team Four Yard and talked to Lieutenant Iverson; he was the CO of Team Four. I told him I wanted to be in Team Four.

"What did Fane say about this?"

I said, "It was his idea."

A few minutes later Lieutenant Iverson said to me, "Fane wants to see you."

I went to see Lieutenant Commander Fane and he asked, "What in the hell do you think you're doing?"

"You told me to resolve this matter myself. I don't want to be in Team Two. I like the men in Team Four better."

Fane said, "OK, Togna, have it your way. But you can't come back here if you don't like it over there."

I said, "I know that, sir."

The second class of trainees had started two weeks ago. They were in their hell week when I joined Team Four. Some thought I was a new trainee starting late. I did not go through hell week again, but I got awakened when they would go on those late-night or early-morning hikes out the main gate. What was left of the training class bunked downstairs with Team Four. There weren't that many men left in the second class. There were about fifty men in the second class after hell week.

Now that I was a regular UDT Four member I had different duties than I had as a trainee. If there wasn't any work detail to do we could go and work out with the trainees. Now I had a choice: isn't that great?

I got friendly with Altieri; he was a coxswain of one of our four small boats. I was sent with six other men to the small-boat landing school at Little Creek for about two weeks to learn to be a coxswain (finally). In school we learned the functions of the boats and the motors and how to fix small breakdowns. When we were taken in to the beach to practice running onto the beach and backing off, as we all took our turn at it, the instructor made the comment that I had a natural feel for boat handling. (He should know.) I said nothing of my experience with Hart aboard ship or the landings of the marines in the Caribbean when I was aboard ship.

Most of the instructors for the second class were still from Team Four and some from Team Two. There were about a dozen men, including myself, who were free from helping with the training. We were given work projects of getting our boats and rubber boats, rubber suits, and winter clothing together and a big list of all kinds of explosive and devices needed for a trip. We packed everything on wooden pallets so they could be loaded aboard ship easily. In between getting all the equipment ready for the trip, we would go to classes on explosives to learn handling of all types and sizes of the stuff. We still did our training, swimming, running, PT. We had everything ready when the second training class was about to finish. The day they were to be taken out for the one mile to swim in for their fins, we old-timers got into a couple of rubber boats to see how many would finish. I don't know how many started the swim, but over thirty finished the swim. Then came some kind of ceremony, standing on

the beach with the fins in one hand and getting a handshake to welcome you into UDT.

I think a lot of the personnel in and around UDT at that time thought that the class that finished around the first of October 1947 was the first class. There was so much going and coming of personnel around April, May, and June of 1947, and only eleven men finished in the first class. There wasn't any paperwork made up to post anywhere to make it official. No pictures were taken, either.

When they were referring to the men who quit during training, they were enlisted men only. Officers never quit; if they got hurt or sick they would get time off to heal or feel better, then resume training. Not all officers went through training.

The mock invasion, with the half-mile explosion in the "Gator," came July 25, 1947. The second class was getting over hell week at that time. Team Four participated in that operation with the help of the Seabees stationed there at Little Creek. With them we made a good impression on the rest of the navy and the marines who came ashore.

I seem to have repeated myself occasionally. I hope I made it clear about the confusion that was going on then.

What kind of ceremony they had for the classes that finished in 1948 and 1949 I don't know. Team Four was away on a trip of some kind either in the Caribbean or Europe when a class finished their training. Team Two took over training the new men. When we came back to Little Creek a few men left for discharge and there would be a few new men who had just finished a class to take their places.

I think the officers had better records than the enlisted men. We were regarded as replacements, just like

a rubber boat, a jeep, or whatever we needed to make up a team. When the inventory got low, just order a few more men.

Sounds like I'm bitchin', well, I'm not! I'm telling you how it was back then. We knew it and accepted it as the way it was. Enough!

Around the middle of October 1947, UDT Four consisted of about eighteen enlisted men, including six of us from the first class, three chief petty officers, five officers, Lieutenant Iverson, Lieutenant Marshall, Lieutenant Anderson, Ensign Richardson, Ensign Jones, and about twenty new men from the second class of trainees. We all boarded the USS *Carpellotti,* APD, for the trip to Newfoundland. I have just two pictures from our training period. I did not have time to take pictures.

25

Good Hiding Place

About forty-six men from UDT Four went aboard the
Carpellotti for the trip to Newfoundland. We were assigned to a division for which we were qualified. I was
assigned topside aft section of the ship. I had to help the
ship's crew with whatever their duties were and stand
watch whenever my turn came.

After that time I thought that every time UDT would
go on a trip this was what UDT did, plus whatever we
were trained for. This was the only time UDT made us a
part of the ship's crew. Every trip after that, on a sub or
a ship, we were passengers and we worked on our own
programs only.

A couple of days out to sea we ran into a nor'eastern,
a big bad storm. We ate peanut-butter-and-jelly sandwiches for four days. The *Carpellotti* was underwater
more than on the surface. About the second day into the
storm, I was on watch and every hour or so I had to unbolt
the hatch, take a look around the aft deck, and report if
anything was loose or lost off the deck. Someone forward
on the ship was doing the same thing. The dog that was
on board the ship got out on the forward deck and was
washed off and washed onto the aft deck. We couldn't
believe our eyes when we saw the dog riding a wave wash
up on the aft deck. Another sailor and myself started to
get the dog. Halfway to him we were knee-deep in sea

water. The sea took him off again. We had a hard time getting back to the hatch, which we left open, and sea water was going into the ship. We got the hatch closed before too much water got inside. We went to the bridge to tell the captain of the ship. They knew; the sailor who opened the forward hatch had told them what happened. They saw us after the dog from the bridge. It was too dangerous to turn the ship; the little ship had to keep heading into the waves or capsize. The whole team was quite upset. We could do nothing but say a prayer. The ship was way off course because we had to keep plowing into the waves. At one time the captain of the ship wanted to know if UDT could blow the arms of the davits that were holding our boats, one set of arms on each side of the ship. Every time we went into the waves, the water was so high on deck it filled the boats with water and it would keep our bow in the water or one of the boats would drain out quicker than the other one so the ship would also roll more than the storm was making us roll. A couple of the older men went out on deck and cut the loading ramps out of the boats so the water could drain out quicker and drain out at the same time to stop some of the roll. We almost capsized a number of times. We would be on our side for long periods at a time. It seemed like the ship would not right itself; then a great big wave struck us and set us straight again. We got through the storm in good shape. We were way off course and had to change direction to catch up with the rest of the fleet.

On this trip we tested the rubber suits in the cold water. We used the rubber suits on every maneuver that we did in the water, on land, and in our rubber boats, with a sub with which we almost collided. We worked at these amphibous operations for about a month.

When we were through with the exercises we went to Halifax, Nova Scotia, for a few days' liberty. Then we were to head home to Little Creek. The first day out to sea heading home after leaving Halifax an announcement was heard over the PA system for all UDT Four men to report to their sleeping quarters and stand by. On the way to our bunks, word was spreading fast that one of the UDT men came on duty drunk. I guessed they were going to confiscate the liquor we had brought aboard ship from Halifax. Almost everyone from UDT had brought a bottle or two on board the ship. I had three bottles in my seabag. They were right at the top of my seabag. When we got to our quarters, Lieutenant Marshall with a baseball bat in his hands was assisted by Lieutenant Anderson and Lieutenant Iverson, our CO. Iverson stood guard as Lieutenant Marshall had us put our seabags in front of us. He took the bat and hit the seabags with the bat. All our clothes and toiletries were in our seabags. If you had a bottle or two of liquor in the seabag, he broke it with the bat, soiling everything with broken glass, too. He got to my seabag and grabbed the top the seabag where I had put the bottles that I had. His hand was right on top of the liquor. He hit my seabag all around; he picked it up and slammed it on deck. He looked at me kind of funny. I gave him one of my shit-eating grins that I got to be famous for while I was in UDT (sometimes I was called Smiley), and he went on down the line hitting all the seabags and breaking bottles as he went. Then he and Lieutenant Anderson came back to me and asked me to lower my bunk. I did. The bunks were fastened to the bulkhead during the day when not in use. Marshall did not see anything. They left, saying they did not want to smell liquor on anyone, or else.

That tiny ship used its galley as a recreation room after supper until taps every day. A day or so after all the clothes were cleaned and the glass picked out of the clothes, everyone was relaxing in the mess hall saying now would be a good time to have a drink. I excused myself and came back in a few minutes with the three bottles that had been at the top of my seabag. "Where did you get this? Where did you hide it?" I never told a soul. It seemed like a good thing to keep a secret for the future. Well! Everyone thought we won; we outfoxed them. After all, they did not get all the liquor. Such little rewards were all we needed to be happy. The liquor helped.

When we got back to Little Creek we went right back to our old routine, running, PT, no swimming, and in between we repaired our equipment that got broken on the trip to Newfoundland. Some of us were sent to a school between amphib operations that the navy had. The team would send around eight to twelve men at a time to a school of some sort, like mine and bomb disposal; some went to deep-sea diving school. Eventually all of us in UDT would attend all the schools needed for our trade.

Every now and then Commander Fane wanted a few men from Team Four to help Team Two with an experiment. It was said at that time "his crazy ideas." I believe some were his ideas and think some were the navy's. Or sometimes we would go on a demonstration that Fane had set up to promote UDT to top brass in the navy. We were always busy. That is one of the reasons that I liked UDT.

The Cavalier Hotel at Virginia Beach was the only hotel there in the 1940s. The rest of the area was woods, summer bungalows, farms, and shacks, only one paved

road to the beach. We were to give a demo and an educational history of why UDTs were important to the navy and the USA to some high-ranking naval officials from Washington, D.C. They were staying at the Cavalier Hotel. There was a rumor that would keep coming up every few months about doing away with the UDTs. In 1947 I think UDT was at its lowest point ever. So this meeting was important. We were to do a cast and recovery off of Camp Pendleton. The weather was bad that week—it rained every day—so the officials decided to leave for Washington at week's end. The UDT officer in charge got permission to use the swimming pool at one end of the pool. We came out of the locker room in swim trunks, knives, face masks, and fins. We also had the forty-pound sacks to carry C-3 or C-4, primer cord, caps, shape charges, and other paraphernalia associated with UDT. Then for the finale, we started at the other end of the pool and swam toward the officials and someone thought that a foot-long piece of primer cord with a cap and a ten-second fuse taped to it and dropped in the pool behind us would give a nice effect. It did. We blew the lights out in the pool. As the officials left, one said, "Too bad the fuse blew out, looked great." After an examination of the pool, we found we'd broken most of the lights in the pool.

These stories I have been telling make it seem like UDT Four did nothing right. We did hundreds of things right. It's just fifty years later looking back, since no one got hurt, it seems funny now. It was serious then.

I went home on leave for Christmas in 1947. I was supposed to be back in Little Creek before the first of January 1948.

That year, a couple of days after Christmas, we had a twenty-seven-inch snowstorm in New York State; it snowed three days. The roads were closed from Albany,

New York City. I called Little Creek and told them I was trying to get back to the base as soon as I could. The roads were not plowed. As soon as the roads were open and the buses were running, I'd start back. I might be a day late. The next day I was able to catch a bus to New York City, then on to Richmond, Virginia, then to Norfolk, Virginia. I was to be at muster at 0800 hours; I got in at 1600 hours, just as everyone who was on base in UDT Four was quitting for the day. Everyone was surprised to see me. They thought I would be a couple of days more getting back. According to the stories about the snow in the papers, the regular bus would have taken longer, but because of the storm there was no schedule. I just made good connections and had a lot of luck.

We got back into the same rigorous routine, all but swimming. We started getting our equipment ready for a trip to the Caribbean to play war games again with the marines. This was about the end of January 1948.

When we arrived at Saint Thomas, one of the Virgin Islands, at an army base, we unloaded the ship and put all of our gear in a warehouse on base. The barracks for the enlisted men was the same design as the one in boot camp, the same as the one we stayed in at Little Creek. Evidently all the barracks built for the Second World War were the same way for the enlisted men.

We started training with the Lambertson lung. We used the Lambertson lung almost every day. We would go island to island, each day a new island. The boat would bring us to about half a mile offshore; then we would swim in to the beach underwater by compass. Then we would go up the beach and over the dune line for our reconnaisance work. Most of these islands were very small, some two or three acres to ten to fifteen acres.

Most of the islands were unoccupied. There were dozens of these islands all over the ocean in the Caribbean.

One day we were doing our usual beach reconnaissance work on one of the small islands. When we got in to the beach in about three feet deep of water we would stand up to count heads to see if everyone made it in. Not far from me there was a man with a baseball bat in his hands standing up to his waist in the water. I said to him, "Take it easy with that bat. You don't have a chance in hell. We have half a ton of TNT in our boat." He said he was not out here to challenge us. From his house on the hill we looked like octopi swimming by. Every once in a while some octopi would swim by and he would get his bat and come down from his house and kill a few for food. They were good eating, he said. They were about due to come by again, for he had not seen them for a few days. When they did come, they came about this time of day, but it could be between six to ten days. It had been a week since he had seen any. We visited with him for a couple of hours. He brought us up to his house. It had four rooms, with very little furniture. He lived alone. It reminded me of being back on the farm, outhouse and all. He had a rowboat stowed halfway from the beach to the house; that was his only way to get to another island. He would catch rainwater from the roof for cooking and drinking. We left saying we would be back again tomorrow at this time to see the octopi.

When we went back the next day we brought two five-gallon cans of fresh water and two five-pound packages of cheese and a few loaves of bread. This man lived all by himself and lived off the land and out of the sea. The island was maybe three acres, just the one house in the middle of the island on top of a hill, so he could see all around the island and all the beaches. After we visited

173

with him for a while it was apparent that the octopi were not coming by today. We said good-bye; maybe we would come by again tomorrow. We got into our boat and started to head for another island to explore. We were looking back at the island and waving good-bye to him. He would not stop waving. We cut the engine and could hear him hollering, waving his arms, running back to the beach. We turned the boat around and went back to the beach. I don't know what you call a bunch of octopi in the water. It looked like a couple of hundred of them, from one foot to three feet from the end of one arm to the end of the arm on the opposite side of the octopus. We caught a few for this man, and then we played around with some of the others. We would let them wrap their arms around us, and then we would grab the end of their arms and pull their arms off our bodies. When you walked to the shallow water and they were out of the water and you pulled their arms off of your body, the suckers on the underside of their arms that they hold onto with would make a popping noise like popcorn a-popping. We played with them for an hour or so; then Lieutenant Anderson said, "Let's go find another island to explore," and away we went.

We did a lot of swimming while on Saint Thomas, with and without the lung units. Instead of running every day, on alternate days we would play softball late in the afternoon, about twelve men on each team. The pitcher was instructed to throw the ball so you could hit it; we would play for a couple of hours. The score would be somewhere in the nineties or over one hundred runs per game.

From the Saint Thomas army base where we were staying while training, over a little hill in back of the barracks there was a cove about a quarter of a mile away.

We used to practice swimming and setting off one-half-pound charges of TNT in our maneuvers. They had just finished building a new hotel not too far from where we were practicing our games, swimming and setting off explosives. I think the hotel was called the Blue Moon. Most of its clientele were people coming from the States to establish residence to get a divorce. They had to live there for at least six weeks.

Across the road all over the place there was coral, right up to the water's edge. One of the owners talked with our officers in charge, asking them to use the beach area in front of the hotel for one of our operations and blast the coral off the beach and he would give us a party at the hotel. We set everything up and a day later we swam in just like any other maneuvers we would do and set up our charges, swam back out to sea, got picked up by our boats, and waited for the explosion to clear the beach. We did this just like we were trained, as if this were an enemy beach. Well!? The explosion was shocking; we blew sand, coral, and water all over the place, and you could not see the hotel after all the debris fell. We couldn't figure out how we overestimated the amount of TNT to use. We blew all the windows out of the front of the hotel. Then we found out later that some of the older men in UDT, our former instructors, had borrowed a truck from the army and loaded the beach with TNT the night before. The owners of the hotel gave us a party anyway. A good time was had by all.

We continued to the end of March, loaded all our equipment on board the *Carpellotti,* and headed home to Little Creek.

It's funny I say home. The navy was my home for almost three and a half years. So wherever I was living, eating, working, and sleeping, it was home. The longest

home I had until I got married was the navy. I lived with my parents on and off a couple of years at a time. I was in an orphanage for a couple of years. I lived with strangers for a year or two at a time while I was growing up. So it was very easy for me to be at home wherever I was.

We arrived in Little Creek early in April 1948. We started in with our regular routine, running, PT, no swimming yet, as the water was too cold. Within a week, six of us were sent to deep-sea diving school, to Portsmouth Navy Shipyard for five weeks. For the first time we actually had books to read and a test at the end of the diving school course. I did very well and have a certificate to prove it. The six of us from UDT passed with high grades. We graduated as second-class deep-sea divers. In 1948, the navy had 1 master diver, 4 chief divers, 10 first-class divers, and, including this class that finished in the spring of 1948, 200 second-class deep-sea divers. There were a couple more men in the class who were going through for the second time.

While we were in diving school an anchoring buoy from the shipping channel broke loose and floated out to sea. The Coast Guard towed it back to the Portsmouth shipyard; they put a new chain on it and needed divers to attach it to the concrete anchor at the bottom of the Chesapeake Bay channel in water 200 feet deep. The chief diver at the school asked MacAllister and me if we would like to assist him in hooking the buoy to the anchor. Mac, Cook, and I worked a lot together under water with our shallow-water equipment. Mac and I showed eagerness and enthusiasm to get at the job. A tug brought the barge with the diving equipment on board out to the site. There were other experienced divers and tenders onboard. The rest of the class came along, too. They were to observe the operation. The three of us got suited up

with what they called hard hats, brass helmets, and deep-sea diving suits. The three of us are lowered to the bottom of the channel; it took a while to find the concrete slab with the other end of the broken chain. We removed the broken chain and hooked up the new chain. Everything went smoothly; the chief diver was impressed with the way Mac and I just went right to work. I think that little job got Mac and me the highest score in the class.

When we got back to Little Creek from diving school we found out we had volunteered for lifeguard duty. Our names were submitted for lifeguard training. The commander of the base at Little Creek thought it proper that UDT men be lifeguards. The UDT personnel had a few privileges more than the regular men on base at Little Creek. (Of course, we all volunteered.)

There were two sections of beach at Little Creek Amphib Base in the Chesapeake Bay. They were set aside for recreation for navy personnel, one for enlisted men and the other for officers and their families. After passing our test and being given our lifeguard patches, everyone wanted to be lifeguard at the officers' beach. That was short-lived for UDT Four lifeguards; UDT Two had the job all to themselves. UDT Four had to pack up for another trip to somewhere. All we were told was we would be gone for about three months. There weren't any winter clothes among our gear and equipment that we packed for the trip. Looking at the equipment, we knew our destination was somewhere warm; we figured the Gulf of Mexico, like the Panama Canal Zone!

A few days before we were to leave for our trip, the commodore of the base wanted to see us off, so we had to get all spruced up for an inspection. We were all lined up singly on the street in front of our building, the "warehouse." The commodore arrived with two captains, two

lieutenants, and a couple of petty officers. As they came around the end of the line to begin inspection of us, I caught a side view of the commodore. Everyone was talking until he stepped into view. I had, and still have, a habit of saying a derisive remark or two under my breath that only a few people close to me should hear. He was maybe fifty-five or so years old and fat, had a big belly, and was breathing so hard I could hear him as he waddled around the end of the line to begin his inspection of UDT Four. I said under my breath, "Christ! What a perfect specimen to represent UDT." Well! Everybody stopped talking, no one moved, and I guess everyone in the area heard my whisper. It was very quiet. The commodore started down the line very slowly, looking over each man carefully. When he came to me he stopped in front of me and looked me straight in the eye. I stared back and neither he nor I blinked. (The thought that was going through my mind was, *Three days bread and water in the brig.*) I smiled. It was probably a shit-eating grin.

He said to me, "Are they your teeth?"

I said, "Yes, sir!"

He raised his right hand toward my mouth. I didn't flinch a muscle. Then he stopped and he went to his teeth and removed his upper plate and he said to me, "Can you do that?"

I said, "No, sir."

He said, "Show me."

I pulled on my teeth.

The commodore said, "You have nice teeth. Take care of them."

I said, "Yes, sir," and he went on down the line looking us over carefully.

After he left, we changed back to our work clothes and started loading the equipment on trucks to bring it

to the ship at Norfolk Naval Base, the USS *Pocono,* a flagship with a vice admiral onboard, Donald Bradley Duncan.

By the time we loaded all our equipment onboard, we knew we were going to the Persian Gulf.

26

Always on the Caret

We crossed the Atlantic Ocean to Gibraltar in six or seven days, no storms. We had an incident a couple of days after we left Norfolk. This ship was big; after breakfast we would run from bow to the stern of the ship up one side, back on the other side. We would do this an hour or so, then PT. After lunch the same thing. We did this every day. This one day we were cruising quietly in the ocean, the water was smooth, looked like it was glass. Lieutenant Anderson was our executive officer and our PT leader. He had us doing calisthenics at midship. After a half hour or so a messenger from the bridge told Lieutenant Anderson we had to stop whatever we were doing. It's hard to believe that calisthenic exercises in union would set up such a unique rhythm that it would make a large ship like the *Pocono* rock and roll so that the personnel onboard the ship could not walk without stumbling. We still did our exercises, with smaller groups and in different places throughout the ship.

We stayed two days at Gibraltar so everyone could go ashore, half the ship's crew at a time. The Rock of Gibraltar is honeycombed with tunnels, man-made and natural caverns. We spent most of our day on the rock. We could not go to Spain. There was a heavy fence at the border, all overgrown with vines. We had to pull the foliage away to see through to Spain. We stopped into a

bar to get a drink of beer; they had light and dark beer. The beer was served to us at room temperature. It had a nice head of foam on top of a beer mug, about sixteen ounces. We thought their cooler was out of order, so I went to the bartender and told him our beer was warm. He laughed; that's the way it was served here. He had a little charcoal burner with a few iron pokers in it. They were red-hot. He said, "Bring your mug over here." I returned with my beer. He put the hot poker in my beer for a second or two, then said, "Now drink." I did. It tasted really good. We spent the rest of the day there. When we boarded the ship, we felt no pain.

The next stop was Naples, Italy. We had to anchor in the Bay of Naples; the port was cluttered with many sunken ships. They were sunk during the Second World War. When we anchored in Naples Bay for liberty one of the LCPS' landing craft personnel boats like ours that was used for bringing men ashore was malfunctioning. Mr. Anderson asked me to see if I could fix it. He was our Executive Officer of UDT 4 on this trip. Most of us in UDT went to motor mechanic school on these type of boats. I climbed over the side of the ship and walked out on the swinging boom to where the boats were tied up. I climbed down a swing ladder into the LCP. I remove the cover at the stern of the LCP so I can crawl into the compartment to where the filters are. From past experience, the way the LCP sounded and was acting, it could be the filters. I change the filters. I see now why the ship's mechanics could not fix their own boats—they did not want to go into the bilge. The water was dirty—half was oil and grease. As I crawled out of the bilge area, I reached up and grabbed the side of the opening to pull myself out. My hand full of grease and oil came to rest on the end of our American flag. It was swinging in the

breeze when I went in and now part of the flag was laying on the opening of the hole. I did know this until I pulled myself out of the bilge. Now I'm moving the flag so it won't get anymore oil or grease on it. I find a rag and clean up the area, cover the hole, start and run the engine to see if everything is working. I get a cheer from a few sailors watching me on deck. The engine sounded great, now I go to our quarters to get cleaned up and ready for liberty in Naples.

I'm on deck with Cain to get our liberty cards to go ashore. The officer of the day says my card was pulled. I am restricted to the ship. I try to find Lt. Arseneault, he is our CO. He has gone ashore already. I go to the officers section on the ship, which is off limits to enlisted men, to find Lt. Anderson. I find him. He reminds me that I am in a restricted area. I want to know why my liberty card was pulled. Lt. Anderson says one of the first-class boatswain mates put me on report for soiling the American flag. He says I used the flag as a rag to wipe my hands with and Lt. Anderson shows me the soiled flag. I told Lt. Anderson what happened and that it was not done on purpose. I remind him that the ship's crew did not like us on their ship and if I used the flag as a rag, it would have a hell of a lot more grease and oil on it. The bilge of these small boats are all filled with oil and grease. They present a fire hazard.

"I would like to make out a report stating that fact, Sir."

"Togna—forget about it, here is your liberty card, I will bring this up to the ship's Captain."

"What are you doing with my liberty card?" I asked. "The only safe place for your card was with me. I knew you would be looking me up, I wanted to hear your side of the story."

"Thank you," I said.

I found Cain and off we went on liberty, on the same boat that caused all the trouble. I'm Italian and I almost did not go ashore in Naples.

We stayed four days in Naples. On the first day we went cruising around the different points of interest. A couple stand out in my mind. One was Soldiers Park, out in the countryside a few miles out of Naples, acres and acres of white crosses. It was the burial ground of World War Two servicemen from both sides of the war. The other was Mount Vesuvius, where we climbed to the top of the volcano and looked down into the crater. It was cooking! Steam was coming up out of the ground, six or seven points all around the bottom of the crater. It was about three hundred feet down (or is that the top?). We got really dirty from the climb, volcanic ash all over the place. We had our dress whites on; we went back to the ship.

The next day we decided to stay in Naples. As we walked around the city, it was in near-extinction. The city of Naples had a ruinous air about it as we walked block after block; there were piles of rubble three stories high. Every once in a while we would come to a section where everything was intact. We had noticed while walking signs bearing the name of TOGNA were all over the city, like the name Smith in the USA.

We walked into a restaurant to have something to eat at the end of the day that had the name TOGNA hanging over the door. There were many business signs with TOGNA on them. We ate, drank wine, and enjoyed a great meal. When we went to pay the bill, I mentioned my last name was the same as the name on the front of the restaurant. I showed the women who was to take the money my liberty card with my name on it. They started to talk

to each other in Italian. They wouldn't take any money; in fact, they gave us a few bottles of wine. We were feeling no pain then. We went down to the dock to catch our motor launch back to the ship; it was 2300 hours. We drank one of the bottles of wine while waiting for the launch for the trip back to the ship. We couldn't drink any more. Cain said "Throw the rest of them anyway." I said, "No! I'll take them." I couldn't throw them away; they were a gift. When we got to the ship while we were still in the launch, I put a bottle in each of my socks, one on each foot. My buddies thought I was crazy. The gangway is a set of metal steps from water level to the top deck alongside the ship. The deck seemed like a hundred steps away; it was more like forty. Halfway up the steps, the bottles in my socks stretched the socks so the bottles were hitting the metal steps as my foot did. The rest of the way up there it was Togna *klunk klunk*. I got to the officer's deck with the bottles still in my socks. I asked the officer on duty for permission to come aboard, as everyone did. He gave everyone permission but me.

He asked me my name. I said, "Togna, sir."

"What division are you from? He had the seaman on duty with him writing this down.

I said, "UDT, sir."

He pondered a few seconds, took the papers from the clipboard the sailor was writing on and crumpled it in his hand, then said to me, "Togna, I'm going to turn my back. I want to hear two splashes over the side; then you will be welcome aboard." I took the two bottles from my socks and put them in my pants by my waist, under my jumper. I took my shoes off and threw one.

The officer said, "That is only one splash."

I threw the second shoe over, and he said, "You are welcome aboard."

I said, "Good night, sir." I turned quickly and ran down the deck to our quarters. The seamen on duty with the officer saw what I did; he did not say anything.

I don't know why I did these crazy things. Whenever I did anything and when I was questioned, I never made an excuse or implicated anyone. I took the blame.

The next port of call was Athens, Greece. Our visit was two days. We went to see the Acropolis, the Temple of Olympus, the Temple of Hephaestus, and a few other places of interest that do not come to mind now. At the end of the day we ended up in a restaurant to eat and drink, then back to the ship by midnight.

Next port, Izmer, Turkey, for two days. We went sightseeing around the countryside most of the day. We were well received in Turkey; the people liked Americans. I think it was because we gave Turkey a lot of relief money.

Military service was compulsory in Turkey. Every male had to serve three years in the army or navy. Maybe this was where our Congress got the idea from when they tried to do this in the United States after the Second World War.

Everything was controlled by the Turkish government. There wasn't much to do for nights in Izmir; we went back to the ship early.

As we continued on our trip to the Suez Canal, Port Said, Egypt, was at the entrance point to the Red Sea by the Suez Canal. There was no law enforcing in the city of Port Said. The police looked the other way; the city was dangerous. We did not stop for a visit. We continued through the Red Sea to the Gulf of Aden, on in to the Arabian Sea. In the Arabian Sea, the water was calm, but there were giant swells that had about a half a mile between them. As the ships were sailing on to the Gulf

of Oman in line, following each other, the ship behind us sometimes would be down in a valley of water. It looked like two small mountains, one on each side. The ship looked to be eight hundred to one thousand feet below us, and then within three or four minutes, the *Pocono* would be down in the valley of water and the other ship would be on top of the mountain of water. This was a fascinating and interesting phenomenon to witness. On top of this, our ship stopped dead in the water; we were floating around in the water like a giant cork. UDT was summoned to the davits, one on each side of the ship, in our swim trunks. We were going to run a cast and recovery out in the middle of the Arabian Sea . . . in this crazy water.

Evidently the officers were having their lunch served to them out on the top deck like they often did in good weather and calm seas. I'm sure they had a cocktail before, during, and after lunch. To them up there it was a perfect viewing stand. The boats were lowered full of UDT men with fins and in swim trunks. We were cast off in the water in line, and at times we would be down in the valley of water so that we would only see the swimmers in the water. We did not see the boat that let us off or the other ships. Talk about a lost and lonely feeling; it looked like the walls of water were going to swallow you up. As the water looked like it was going to dump on you, you floated like a cork about four or five seconds. Later you were on top of the wave and you could see everybody in the water and all the ships and our two LCPRs running around like two water rats. Talk about a thrill! As you kept going up and down with the water it felt like you were on a giant roller-coaster ride. At times we were so high in the water and the *Pocono* was so low, we could actually look down into the smokestack. We had to be

three hundred to four hundred feet above the ship at times, and vice versa. We went to the other ships and did our act for them, too. Then back to the *Pocono* one more time for the vice admiral, then back aboard ship and on our way to the Persian Gulf.

Prior to that afternoon stint in the Arabian Sea, the men aboard the *Pocono* did not like us UDT. We were navy, they were navy, but we had a few more privileges than they had on their ship. After this exercise, the other men admired us; they thought we were crazy, but they liked us. A few of the ship's men said, "You know, you guys could have drowned out there. The bottom of the ocean at this point is over a mile deep." We responded, "Hell, you could drown in two feet of water!"

On in to the Persian Gulf to Kuwait. We docked in Kuwait for a couple of days, just for a quick visit. Went into town. What a beautiful city; everything was bright and clean, water fountains all over the place. There was a masonry wall all around the city. On the other side of this wall was sand as far as you could see, just a big wasteland out there.

Now it was time to go to work. The ship moved out into the gulf and anchored, and every day we would leave the ship after breakfast with a packed lunch for the beach and start to record the depth of the gulf from shoreline to about three miles out into the gulf. Some of us recorded the height of the sand and dunes from the water's edge inward until we met either an army or marine engineer surveying the dunes. Every couple of days the ship would pull anchor and move a few miles down the gulf. We surveyed almost all of the western coast of the Persian Gulf next to Saudi Arabia. We were in the gulf about three weeks in the month of August 1948; the temperature was near 100 degrees Fahrenheit every day. Onboard ship

with all that iron around you, it would get to 135 degrees Fahrenheit in the daytime. Everyone aboard ship had prickly heat rash, except for most of UDT. We left the ship early in the morning and did not return until evening. Even though on shore it got very hot in the sand, we would be in the water a couple of times a day.

After a few days of surveying, we were eating our lunch as usual and a few Arabs came around to see what was going on and started to chatter at us, pointing their fingers at us. We inquired from a British soldier who accompanied us each and every day with armed rifles. He interpreted what they were saying to us. He said, "They are saying Americans are a dirty people. They eat food with their right hands." All these Mideastern countries are very poor, they don't have toilet paper or soap, so any dirty job is done with the right hand and anything that is to be eaten is put into the mouth with the left hand. We used to tease them by feeding each other with our right hands. They would walk away in disgust at us Americans.

While we were off the Arabian coast, the Emir of Arabia came aboard our ship for a formal visit, His Highness Abdul Mukis Bin Jilur. He was accompanied by several rifle-carrying guardsmen. Everybody onboard ship was on their best behavior.

Our work done, we started back "home" to Little Creek. Back through the Red Sea, the Mediterranean Sea, and back across the Alantic Ocean. We did not stop at any port. We arrived in Little Creek around the middle of September 1948.

27

Close Calls

We started in as usual on our regular routine, running, PT, and swimming. Whenever we were not at a school or on a maneuver, we always did our running and PT every day. About a week after coming back from the Persian Gulf, over half of Team Four packed up to fly to New London, Connecticut, to the submarine school for about three weeks. We flew about four to five hundred feet above the ocean from Norfolk, Virginia to New London, Connecticut.

The plane was a Second World War leftover. It flew in the air like a truck running over a bumpy road. The air went through the plane like a sieve. There were no doors, just a chain across the opening so you would not fall out easily.

In New London, we trained in the 100-foot water tank, about 20 feet in diameter. It looked like a big silo. We were working the decompression chamber, too. We would work under pressure to simulate living in a submarine and the 100-foot water tank to simulate leaving a sub at a depth of 100 feet without any diving equipment on. We would drift to the surface, which was called a free ascent. We would practice these procedures over and over for days. We flew back to Norfolk on the same plane. When we got off the bus at Little Creek, we were told not to unpack, for we are going to Newfoundland again. We

had a couple of days to do our laundry and get our gear in order. When we got to Newfoundland this time we left the ship and worked from an army base in Argentia. We tried to use our rubber suits off a submarine underwater; they were too bulkly in the escape chamber. So the sub pulled us in a rubber boat to a point; then we would go on our maneuver as planned, come back, and find the sub to complete our objective. We worked with the sub and our rubber boats in the Placentia Bay for a couple of weeks. Sometime during the day we would hike in the mountains on Avalon Peninsula. One day we hiked to Saint John's on the Atlantic coast from Argentia Army Base; it was over fifty miles. The ship we came to Newfoundland on was in port there. The ship took us back to the army base, we loaded our gear onboard, and the next day we headed to Little Creek. This trip to Newfoundland did not produce the results our officers wanted while we were working off the submarine with our winter gear on. They didn't realize how clumsy and awkward things would be. Well! That's why we went out and practice.

After a few weeks back at Little Creek from Newfoundland, eight of us UDT Four men were sent to Aberdeen, Maryland, to mine and bomb disposal school for two weeks. This was about the first of December 1948. I did not go home for Christmas in 1948. I had used the time to go home with Clemensen to Detroit, Michigan, earlier in the year. His parents were wonderful people. I had a great time in Detroit.

For the next month or so we did our regular routine. Every once in a while UDT Two would ask for anywhere from four to ten men to assist them in doing a work program or a demo or even a school of some sort. The navy had these training exercises all the time, and every now and then if we had time on our hands a half-dozen or so

men from UDT would be sent. I usually was one of the men to go.

Lieutenant Marshall and Lieutenant Anderson were always after me to take a test for my next rate. I would say, "I'm not interested. I'm going home when my hitch is up." Every week either Lieutenant Anderson or Lieutenant Marshall would remind me to take my test for seaman first class. I would not take the test. One day Lieutenant Anderson had me come to the office. Within a few minutes Lieutenant Marshall and Lieutenant Anderson started asking me questions. I stood there for a minute, puzzled. I asked, "What did I do now that I'm being interrogated on?"

They both said together, "Nothing. We just want to know if you can answer these questions."

I said, "Yes," and for about half an hour they took turns asking me questions.

Then Lieutenant Anderson said to Lieutenant Marshall, "That should do it."

I asked, "Do what?"

"You just passed the seaman first-class test. Sign these papers."

I did and went back to my work party. I said nothing to anyone.

When we would go on a work detail Joe DiMartino usually was the petty officer in charge. Joe was an easygoing guy. The first couple of times that we went on details with DiMartino he was lackadaisical about everything, so we goofed off. Ensign Jones asked us one day how we were coming along with the work. DiMartino said we should be done in a few more days.

Ensign Jones said, "It was only about two days work to start with. I will check with you later."

We were moving ammunition supplies around in a warehouse, actually a magazine covered with earth. When Ensign Jones showed up, he asked, "How many cases of this" or "how many of these do we have?" We were supposed to be taking inventory and stocking everything in order.

I said to Ensign Jones, "It will be done tomorrow."

After Ensign Jones left I got on the forklift and started moving the TNT around and stocking what should be together and told a few guys to get some paper and start counting inventory. Everybody in the work party got involved. After that, anytime I went on a work party, with whoever was in charge, I always asked the officer who ordered the work to be done what was to be done. When we got to the site, I started to work; some of the men would join me, and the others would stupidly wait to be ordered to move a box from here to there when it was obvious where it had to go. Most of the men in UDT were enlisted men and just seamen, a few third-class petty officers, and a few more second-class petty officers, a couple of first-class petty officers, and a couple of chief petty officers. Most of the time in UDT it didn't matter who had rank; we were trained to work together even with our officers. None of us wore clothing with insignias while working or practicing maneuvers. We would respect rank when one had his uniform on, designating so.

One time on a work party, one of the new men (a trainee) was reluctant to do any work. He said to a few other UDT men, "Togna is only a seaman first class and I'm a third-class boatswain mate." He came over to me and said I should be taking orders, not giving them.

I said, "Go see DiMartino. Joe is off somewhere nice and quiet studying for a first-class exam."

The kid came back and said, "I'm in charge."

I said, "OK," and kept on working.

After a few hours everything seemed to be done; now what do to do next? (I can't think of the kid's name. Anyway, he wasn't around long.) We were standing around and goofing around; a couple of the guys (UDT men) said to me, "Don't you think we ought to start squaring away the next building?"

"I'm not making suggestions anymore."

"Yeah, I guess we are outranked."

This kid went to see DiMartino to find out what to do next (which was proper). DiMartino told him, "When you don't know what to do, go see Togna."

This kid came back to the work party and said, "Look, I'm new here. What do we do now?"

We went to the next building and started to work. This UDT Four team in 1948 was a good group of men. We were all Indians and we were all chiefs. We worked well together. It didn't matter whose idea it was; if it looked good to the rest of us, that's the way we did it. I got the name as being in charge only because I started to work first. I just could not stand around doing nothing where there was something to do.

On with business. Every week or so Lieutenant Anderson or Lieutenant Marshall would remind me to study for my next rate. I would keep telling them, "I'm not making the navy my career."

They engaged James T. Cook and Thomas McAllister to persuade me to study for a test. Cook would say, "Togna, with no schooling, what kind of job could you get outside?"

I would say, "I don't know," but it didn't matter because I was going to be in some kind of business of my

own. I said to Cook and Mac that I wanted to be a million-aire and staying in the service I didn't have a chance in hell. McAllister would start when Cook got exhausted. The three of us were quite friendly and shared some of our personal affairs with one another. We were like brothers, giving one another hell and trying to give one another advice. Anyway, this was an ongoing thing. McAllister was best man when Cook got married and I was one of the ushers.

Around this time, late in 1948, UDT Two and UDT Four had taken over the brig building and yard. It had a fence all around the building and bars in the windows so no one could break out or break in; that's what UDT wanted. Cook and a few more men from UDT Two and Four were selected to work on a secret project. All the chief petty officers were involved, about twelve men in all. While I was still in the service, Mack and I would ask Cook what was going on in the brig. All Cook would say was in time we would all know. I never did find out while I was in service. On one of my visits to Little Creek to see Cook with my wife and two children in the early sixties, Cook took us down to a restricted area at Little Creek and showed us the capsule that the astronauts would be coming back to Earth in. They were planning what to do as early as 1949. Then I put together other events that went on at that time: the time we went to the New London sub base, the times we spent in the pressure chambers. In the summer of 1949 Fane had a half-dozen of us jump into the ocean from a helicopter from about forty feet above the water, about the height of an aircraft carrier deck. That one did not make sense to us at all. We were going into the beach for reconnaissance or to set charges on an enemy beach. We were supposed to be quiet and sneak in and out. I think a lot of things we did that

some of us thought were crazy were experiments and doing all kinds of tests that were incorporated with our work. Later when I met Cook and the space program was in full swing, it was public knowledge. Cook and the rest of the men in the brig were keeping records of how things worked out. This is all speculation, but it did make sense to me. They kept records to help the space program that was going on then to gather valuable information.

This winter in Norfolk was an unusually cold winter. We had a couple of snowfalls that were four and six inches deep. They rarely get snow in Norfolk. We had a few guys who never saw snow. They went nuts rolling in the stuff (1948 and 1949).

On the way to the movies one night, Clemensen, Cain, and I stopped by the gym (it was on the way) to see McAllister and Cook working out lifting weights. Mac always wanted to compete in a weight-lifting meet anywhere. Cook and Mac were always after me to join them in lifting weights. They had a bar set up, and Mac was about to lift it over his head. It was 250 pounds (which I didn't know). It looked like nothing, a couple of weights on each end of a bar. Mac had his hands on the bar, his feet were stamping, and he was snorting and grunting, trying to lift the barbell of 250 pounds. He got it up waist high and dropped it.

I said, "Get out of the way." I stepped over to the 250-pound barbell. I grabbed it and lifted it up over my head with one motion. I didn't drop it. I brought it down to my waist; then I placed it on the floor. Well! Mac was going on something terrible! About how I did it all wrong, that was not the way to do it.

In the meantime, Cook was trying to chime in, saying to Mac, "Togna here just lifted two hundred and fifty pounds."

"My god, that's right!" Mac said.

Then they started in again, trying to get me to lift weights with them. I said to Cook and Mac, "Clemensen and Cain and I are late for the movies," and we left. That wasn't the last of it.

The next day Commander Fane sent word to UDT Four he wanted to see Togna as soon as possible. Commander Fane had gotten hold of an Italian one-man submarine and a lot of paperwork, all in Italian. He asked me if I could translate this material for him.

I said, "I can't write or read or speak Italian. I never did learn how to."

He didn't believe me; his reason was that they heard me cuss in Italian.

I said, "That's all the Italian I can remember. As a kid I lived in an Italian ghetto in Mahopac, New York. When I was very young we lived with my grandmother for a few years, and that's all they spoke in the house, Italian."

When I went to first grade I could hardly speak English. I remember I could not read anything in English. I was made fun of by the other kids in the first grade. By Halloween I was speaking English and reading "see Dick run." I've always told people I forgot what Italian I knew. As a six-year-old, how many words did I know? Commander Fane believed I was getting even with him for not helping me get to the bottom of the twenty dollar fiasco months ago. I never carried a grudge; whatever happens, happens, and that's the way life is. I've always made the best of a situation and looked at the bright side of things. It's learning how to live.) I was told this by one of the officers a few days later, as he tried to get me to look over the papers. I said, "You don't believe me, either." I said a few cusswords in Italian to him and said, "I can't even spell them, either!"

196

The early part of January 1949, half of the team started to pack gear for a trip to Saint Thomas, about twenty men with two officers, Lieutenant Arseneault as CO and Lieutenant Anderson as XO. We were going to board a submarine at St. Thomas for a couple of weeks and conduct maneuvers from the sub with the Lambertson lung. The other half of the team was going somewhere else.

We would not have any liberty until we got back from Saint Thomas. There was nothing there, and we were kept busy. So, a half-dozen of us planned a weekend in Norfolk. I usually could talk my way out of a jam if something was to come up unexpectedly. So I was chosen to go into town early on Friday to rent a room and buy a half-dozen bottles of whiskey from the state-run liquor store. The liquor store run by the state was open from 10:00 A.M. until 5:00 P.M. Monday to Friday. I would leave after lunch on Friday. I got my liberty card from Dietrick, who was our yeoman (secretary) at that time, and the rest of the guys would cover for me and make some kind of excuse if need be. Our workday was not over until 5:00 P.M., so whenever we wanted any liquor we had to buy it black-market and it was twice the price of the liquor store.

It was about seven Friday night by the time Clemensen, Cain, Alticri, and a couple more men I can't name were at the hotel with me. We went out to eat. The next day after a late breakfast we started to hit the bars. The only drinks you could buy over the bar were beer and wine. We used to bring a bottle of liquor with us and spike our beer. All the bars were filled with sailors, soldiers, and marines. Around the middle of the day on Saturday, everyone in the bar (we decided to stay put) was in good spirits, playing shuffleboard and playing darts.

The jukebox was loud; everyone was having a good happy time. We were going south to warm weather on Wednesday and teasing the men who were staying in Norfolk and Little Creek this winter.

I was playing shuffleboard and doing well. Cain came up to me and said a sailor on the other end of the bar (the bar was shaped like a large horseshoe) would not let him go to the bathroom to urinate! (Now, if I was verbally telling this story, I would have submitted a few different words here and there.) I shooed Cain away. I was on a winning streak and I didn't want to be bothered. After a while, Cain (he was tiny, four eleven, about 140 pounds) could hold it any longer was begging me to help him get into the bathroom. I excused myself from the shuffleboard and went around the bar with Cain to see what the problem was. The bar on this side was about five feet from the hall that led to the bathroom, and next to the door was a group of sailors. They were having a good time harassing whoever wanted to go to the bathroom; some they intimidated and others they didn't. Cain was small and had a patch sewn on his sleeve indicating he was a frogman. They thought he should swim in his own urine and would not let him in. I was in front of Cain; they started with me. I joked back with the three of them and had them off-guard and Cain skooted by and got into the bathroom. Cain came out and we walked back to the other side of the bar. The three of them were second-class petty officers off a ship that was going south, too. Cain was third-class and I was first-class seaman. The one second-class petty officer was furious that they got outfoxed. He came around the bar and started to raise hell with me. I told him he and his buddies ought to be ashamed of themselves, picking on little Cain. This petty officer was maybe one inch taller and about ten pounds

heavier than I was. I reached for my beer on the bar and before I got the glass to my mouth he sucker-punched me in the jaw. The bartenders all hollered, "Fight outside!"

I walked to the door. The bar had one step down to the sidewalk. It was snowing and freezing rain; the sidewalk and Grandby Street were covered with two inches of wet snow. I slipped on the step as I went outside. I was on my hands and knees, trying to get up on my feet, and this sailor kicked me in the mouth, splitting my upper lip. I wiped my mouth with my right hand, and it was covered with blood. The adrenaline took over the next ten or so seconds. I knocked him back inside the bar. I was standing on the sidewalk looking at the other sailor. He was on his back in the tavern on the floor with glass all around him and some sticking in and out of him. These storefront bars had big plate glass across the front of them from floor to ceiling. This glass had to be twelve feet high by sixteen feet wide. The left side of his face had a piece of glass in it. Then I noticed my left hand was bleeding. After hitting him several times, I did not get my left hand back quick enough when he went through the window and the upper section of glass came down across the back of my hand. My little finger, ring finger, and middle finger were cut to the bone and bleeding bad!

My buddies started hollering, "Shore patrol!" Without thinking, I started to run.

After running a few blocks, I looked back to see if they were following me. In the two-inch-thick slush and snow I was leaving a blood trail a blind man could follow. I turned around and started back to the tavern. A block or so before the bar, the shore patrol, a chief petty officer and a third-class petty officer, came around the corner. The third-class petty officer wanted to handcuff me. The

chief said, "No. You're cut pretty bad." He took my tie from around my neck and used it as a tourniquet around my wrist to stop the bleeding. The chief asked me what happened; I told him as we walked back to the tavern. When we got back to the bar the ambulance was just leaving with the other sailor in it. I started to holler for the ambulance to stop for me. The chief said, "We have another one coming for you." The chief questioned the bartenders and made out his report. He sent the third-class petty officer with me to the Norfolk Naval Hospital to get stitched up, fifteen stitches in my left hand and two stitches in my upper lip. When they were done with me at the hospital, they said I could go. The third-class petty officer was nowhere to be found. I went back to downtown Norfolk to the bar. You would never have known there was a fight or that the glass was broken. Everything was fixed. I found my buddies, and we continued to enjoy ourselves. My left arm was in a sling. Other than the bartenders, who asked how I was, no one knew I was in a fight at this bar. I felt no pain; my arm and upper lip did not hurt at all. Sunday morning I got up sore all over. After breakfast I went back to the base.

Monday morning as we fell in for muster Lieutenant Anderson looked at me (my arm in a sling and puffed-up face) and said, "I hope you are the winner?"

I said, "I am, sir."

He said, "My God! What am I saying? You didn't kill him, did you?"

I said, "No, sir." (I must have looked horrible.)

"Where did you get stitched up?"

"At the naval hospital," I said.

"What are the charges?"

"None, I think!" I said.

200

Lieutenant Anderson said, "I'll read it on the report. Do what you can to help load the equipment onboard ship. We leave Wednesday."

Near the end of the day Lieutenant Anderson came into the warehouse and said, "Togna, we got the report. It seems you were not the troublemaker." Then Lieutenant Anderson said, "Togna, you are going to have to pay better attention in the judo classes from now on."

We loaded everything in the forward hole on the APD *Carpellotti*. Because the ship's crew had to go through the compartment during the day to do their daily task, I was elected to guard the ten ton of TNT and other equipment we had aboard, mainly to see no one would sneak a smoke down here.

When we got to Saint Thomas and everything was stored in the warehouse, to kill time and stay physically fit we played baseball, waiting for the submarine that we were going to spend about three weeks aboard. The sub was supposed to have been waiting for us.

We had two guys in the group of twenty men on this trip who each thought he was the better pitcher. We split into two teams, those who liked Dietrick, he was our new yeoman from the second class, and Sulinski, an oldtimer, a gunner's mate, both third-class petty officers.

I just had the stitches removed by our medic, Chief Boone, and my left arm was in a sling only to remind me I shouldn't do anything strenuous. Lieutenant Arseneault, our CO, was off somewhere to find out what had happened to the sub. That left nine men on each team. Lieutenant Anderson said, "Togna, you are umpire." We started to play ball. About the fourth inning, Lieutenant Anderson came up to bat, I was umpiring behind the catcher, the score is nothing to nothing, and everybody was about to go sleep. The only two playing ball were

the two pitchers. Lieutenant Anderson said to me, "Wake these guys up, will you?"

I said, "I don't have a bell or a horn."

He said, "You are the umpire."

Sulinski threw a ball past Lieutenant Anderson; I hollered, "Strike one!"

Lieutenant Anderson looked back at me with a smile and said, "You don't have to pick on me."

I said, "I'm not picking on you."

Sulinski was happy, a big smile on his face, and threw a perfect strike. I hollered, "Ball one!"

Sulinski went nuts. The rest of the team came to life and started to threaten the umpire. I said I wasn't ready and didn't see the ball coming. Sulinski threw another ball and Lieutenant Anderson got a hit and was on first base. Everyone was raising hell, yelling, "Kill the ump!" Dietrick's team scored two runs before they were put out. Of course, I had to even the score. I did the same thing to Dietrick. Same kind of response with a few more remarks added, like, "He has the stitches in his eyes," and, "Togna is going to have a few more stitches." We were finally in the bottom of the ninth inning; the score was tied at six. Sulinski's team was up at bat, two outs, two men on bases, first and second. Next man hit a grounder out to center field. The ball got to home plate a second after the runner from second base did. I called him out! All hell broke loose. I thought for a minute I was going to get some more stitches. Lieutenant Anderson came to the rescue, saying he saw the same thing I did. Everybody said we both needed glasses. It sure did get the blood moving in these guys. They wanted the game to go into extra innings. I said, "I'm the umpire," and called the game over because of chow time. They talked about the game all night. I had to end the game as a tie. If you are

going to fix a game, that's the way to fix it. Lieutenant Anderson agreed.

Our submarine was dockside when we got up in the morning. After breakfast we loaded what was needed on board and went out into the Caribbean Sea. After a few days of trying to find the sub, submerged in 100 feet of water, by using our wrist compass and the sub trying to track us by radar, we had many failures. We worked day and night to track us by radar, we had many failures. We worked day and night off the sub. One day off of Visques, a few of us were out in the bay with the sub trying different things. The rubber boat we were working in started to leak air. We were transferring the gear to a new rubber boat when the kid in the radar room aboard the sub came running out saying he had something on his screen and lost it. Moving the equipment back and forth from one rubber boat to the other rubber boat, he would get us on the screen. It was finally discovered that when we moved the anchor and raised it to at least waist-high, he could get us on the radar screen. Now, every man in UDT Four was qualified to hold the anchor waist-high for an hour or two, but how do you do a recon with a man standing up in a rubber boat? After many more test runs of different things to attract us to the sub, someone came out of the sub with an umbrella! Yes, an umbrella! Well, that did the trick. We would carry the umbrella and open it up and in a few minutes out of the sea came a sub.

A few days later we went out on a night recon again to test things out. While we were loading the rubber boat with gear, the umbrella was given to a new trainee to take care of. We got into the beach to do our work, rowed back to where we were to meet the sub, asked the trainee for the umbrella, and he said, "What umbrella? I left it

back on the sub. You guys kid around so much I thought it was a joke—submarine, swim gear, water everywhere, everything and everybody is wet. What the hell do we need an umbrella for?" Ha, ha! In those days you were told to do something, no explaining why or what for; you did it. You got on-the-job training. Of course, the sub finally came up, thinking we lost the umbrella.

One day a big whale was seen staying close to the sub. Later it was identified as a blackfish. Fish, hell, it was as big as the sub we were on, if not bigger. We started to chase it, and it would dive and come up behind us. I don't know if we were playing with the fish or it was playing with the sub. We spent the day doing this, trying to get as close to the fish as we could. Finally, the fish didn't come up anymore. It was so big, when it came up from a dive its back was twenty to twenty-five feet above the water and its head was back in the water before its tail came out of the water. It was awesome!

We were schooled in using the Lambertson lung to swim into the beach from two to three miles out, day or night, also in leaving and entering a submarine at 100 to 120 feet below the surface of the Caribbean Sea. On one maneuver at night, James Cook, McAllister, and I were going to practice and time ourselves by leaving a submarine three miles off Vieques at about 100-feet depth (in 1949). The sub had an escape chamber that could hold four men at a time, packed in like sardines. Well, Cook, Mack, and I had our Lambertson lungs on and there was a lieutenant from the submarine who manned the controls in the escape chamber. All the controls were manual; they had to be turned by hand. We had our face masks on and were breathing in the air in our Lambertson lungs and the lieutenant had just his swim trunks on. After the chamber filled with water (by

the way, we had to get into this chamber from the sub through a hatch in the overhead; after entering we had to straddle the hatch cover so it could be closed; the hatch cover became our floor or deck) up to the Lieutenant's chin, we opened the side hatch and ducked out onto the sub's deck. We closed the hatch and the lieutenant forced the water out of the chamber and went back down into the main body of the submarine and waited for us to complete our mission.

Now Cook, Mack, and I swam to the surface to our rubber boat tied to the stern of the sub. On previous maneuvers we had the rubber boats deflated and tied to the sub's deck. It took too long to untie and pump the rubber boat full of air. Next time we tied an inflated rubber boat on deck. When we went to cut it loose, we damn near lost our Lambertson lungs. The boat shot to the surface like a missile; then we had to chase it down. So now (1949) we tied it to the stern of the sub.

We were in the rubber boat. Mack and I were paddling; Cook was coxswain. We paddled as close to the beach as we could so we wouldn't be detected by marine sentries on the beach, then anchored the boat. Cook stayed with the boat. Mack and I swam as close to the waterline as we thought was safe; then, on this trip it was Mack's turn to go ashore. I don't remember if we were to get something or leave something without being detected. I was to wait. If Mack didn't come back at a precise time, I was to either follow him or, if there was activity on the beach, bring what information I had and go back to Cook waiting in the rubber boat. Well, Mack came back in time. We swam back to Cook in the rubber boat. We did this maneuver a number of times, and each time we would do different things to improve and make it easier. Cook had his lung off and stowed it neatly in

the bow of the rubber boat so as not to let water get into it. The Lambertson lung was a self-contained unit; you used pure oxygen and a canister filled with some kind of pellets (I have forgotten the name). If they got wet, they gave off a gas that could be fatal.

Mack and I were now back in the boat with Cook. We paddled out to sea looking for the submerged submarine. As I said before, we would have one hell of a time with a wrist compass. So, on this trip we tied a rope that glowed in the dark. From the top of the coning tower to the deck on the stern of the sub, we could see the rope about seven to eight hundred feet ahead of us. When we got to the sub, one of us would go down and rap three times at the base of the escape chamber. The other two would wait in the boat and tie it to the sub. This time it was my turn to go down. I rapped three times and in a few minutes I got three raps from within the sub. We did it again for kicks. I went back to the surface and let Cook and Mack know. By the time we go back down our lieutenant would be waiting for us with the hatch open.

It was agreed that I would take my Lambertson lung off when I got into the chamber so we could have more room to work the controls and to turn the valves. I got in the chamber and took off my Lambertson lung. Now that I was back in the chamber it didn't matter if water got in the unit. In a few minutes Mack came in. We waited two or three minutes and Cook didn't show. Mack went back out looking around the deck of the sub. We were about one hundred feet below the surface.

Mack came back in the chamber; he didn't see Cook anywhere. He said, "I'll go up to the rubber boat; maybe he's having trouble with putting his Lambertson lung back on."

It's better than five minutes now; the lieutenant talked to the skipper of the submarine, telling him of our problems and not to start the sub yet.

I told the lieutenant, "I'll take a look outside." My Lamberston lung was off and the mask was full of water, so I couldn't use it. At that time in UDT, all frogmen could hold their breath at least four minutes. I went outside and looked around; I didn't see anything or anybody. I came back in the chamber, eager to get some air. I talked a few minutes with the lieutenant. In the meantime, I was ducking outside looking for Cook and Mack.

After a few minutes more, catching my breath, I went out again looking for them. I looked over the side of the submarine and I saw Mack struggling with Cook, trying to bring him up on the deck of the submarine. We were at 100 feet below the surface at night. I got to the side of the submarine, on the edge, and helped Mack pull Cook to the chamber. We got to the hatch. I needed air and I was outside pushing everybody in. Evidently Cook needed air, too. What a hell of a scramble was going on in that hatch, getting into the chamber for air and trying to get the mask off Cook and keeping his head above water. The lieutenant trying to close the hatch, turning the locking device. He was underwater more than we were, reaching between our legs managing to turn whatever valves he had to, to get the water out of the chamber. When the water started to go down in the chamber and got near our knees, Cook finally stopped struggling with us. As we figured, when he stored his Lambertson lung in the bow of the rubber boat somehow water got in his mask and started that chemical reaction with the pellets.

As we kept going on these maneuvers, we got better and better and became experts in our trade.

We stayed on the sub over two weeks, then went to the base at Saint Thomas and worked from the army base until the end of February. Then, the early part of March, we did a few maneuvers from the *Carpellotti,* our APD. About the middle of March we headed to Little Creek. When we got back to Norfolk Naval Base, as the *Carpellotti* was tying up to the pier, Clemensen came running up to me and said, "Togna, come over here!" I went to the side of the ship that was tying up to the pier. Standing on the pier was the petty officer I had the fight with in Norfolk early in January. I went over to a sailor who was part of the ship's crew and asked him if he knew the sailor on the pier. He said, "He is from the second division. He got injured in a fight in Norfolk the weekend before we left to go south. We had to send is personal stuff to the hospital. He was injured pretty bad, so that he had to stay in the hospital for a few weeks."

I said, "You're kidding?"

The sailor commented, "He was the winner. I wonder what the loser looked like."

I didn't say a word. As soon the gangway was lowered, I was the first one down and Clemensen was behind me hollering, "Togna, leave it be!" over and over.

I came up to this sailor face-to-face. I looked him straight in the eye. He seemed to be all right except for a four-inch scar on the left side of his face. I said, "Do you remember me?"

He said, "No."

I said, "I'm the fellow you had the fight with in Norfolk a couple of months ago, you f— —." Then I took my index finger from my right hand and ran it down the length of the scar on his face. He insisted he didn't remember much of that day. I left it at that. Clemensen was relieved. He thought I was going to hit him again

because all the time I was healing in St. Thomas when I bumped my hand I would cuss this guy out for my cuts.

We were not back a week when in early April 1949 about a dozen of us from UDT Four were sent to Annapolis, Maryland, after spending the winter in the Virgin Islands, to put on demonstrations for then-president Harry Truman and some top brass and a few foreign dignitaries. I think we were in the Chesapeake Bay water off Annapolis; anyway, the water was cold! We were there three or four days, putting on a show a day. While running the first cast and recovery run, approaching the beach, we would throw one-half pound charges with fuse and detonators over the side to simulate mortar fire at us. After we threw about half a dozen, the officer in charge called to stop throwing the charges and we had started to get ready to go over the side when Seabee Thomas saw that a new UDT trainee had pulled a fuse at that time and put the live charge back in a box with a half a dozen or so charges in it. Seabee Thomas grabbed the charge and threw it overboard the same side the rubber boat was tied to, with a swimmer in it. The charge cleared the boat and exploded on the surface of the water as the first swimmer went into the water. Well, what was nearly a disaster turned out to be a sensation for the viewers and we were thought to be great. *Sometimes I wondered.* The only two names I can remember on that trip are Clemensen, my swimming buddy, and of course Seabee Thomas. There have to be half a dozen UDT Four sailors around who remember.

Back at Little Creek the old routine again for a couple of weeks. On liberty in Norfolk one night Scollise got into a fight with a big marine. As they are fighting Scollise said to the marine, "You are going to win this fight,

but you are going to know you were in a fight. I'm like a brahma bull. What! I don't tear down! I shit all over."

The marine said, "I quit!"

That's about the time Scollise, Cain, and I decided to race Scollise's racing car in the stock car races at Ocean Beach Race Track. We had to get a permit to race. In order to get this permit, we had to take a test and drive on the track with a trainer five times before we were given a permit. The three of us passed and got our permit. The first race no one wanted to be first, so I volunteered. It wasn't my car, so I was trying to be careful not to dent the car. Well, that's what the race was all about, wrecking your car. I came in seventh with twelve cars in the race. Scollise cried when he saw his car. I'd had it. I gave him enough money to buy what parts he needed to fix the car. I wasn't afraid of anything, I thought! The unknown did not bother me. In racing on that track it seemed all the other drivers were trying to kill me. I did not race anymore. It wasn't long after I quit that Cain and Scollise quit.

About twenty of us were sent to Fisherman's Island for a survival in the rough training. It is an abandoned island across the Chesapeake Bay from Little Creek, in Virginia.

We were on Fisherman's Island, North Chesapeake Bay, to rough it. We had to live off the land with C rations; we ate raw clams for the first time. We were standing on the dock one day and we noticed these big fish swimming by. Dureau and I looked at each other at the same time. We went for the half-block of TNT; we were tired of C rations. The half-pound charge did not kill them; it only stunned them. The fish were swimming around erratically. We jumped in the water and had to

catch the fish with our bare hands. Everyone was hollering, "That one is getting away!" We would swim after a fish; we had to put our hands in their gills to catch them.

For about half an hour it was a hectic time. We would catch one and heave it on to the dock; sometimes one would flop off the dock and we had to heave him on again. It's quite an exciting way to catch fish. We did not get them all, but we had plenty for supper. Our cook went nuts. Baked beans and C rations took a backseat for a couple of days.

While on the island we did all kinds of maneuvers, swimming in the riptides around the island and experimenting with C-2 and C-3. There were some old buildings on the island we blew up, and the pier with the fish on was also blown up.

Cook had a private airplane he and Big John flew over Fisherman's Island while we were there on the weekend and dropped a couple of six-packs of beer. It hit the spot—twice! At the end of the survival period on Fisherman's Island, a number of us swam back to Little Creek, about twenty miles across Chesapeake Bay.

A day or two back, back to the old routine again. It was noticed that someone had misplaced a .45-caliber pistol that was used on patrol. It could not be found. Everyone was restricted to the base, no liberty for anyone until the gun was back or there was an explanation of its whereabouts. The disappearance was discovered on the same day some of us got back from Fisherman's Island. It was now Saturday and a few of us were looking forward to going into town. A few of us were restless, so we decided to sneak off base and go into town, Clemensen, Dureau, I think Reed, and I. The base had a ten-foot Cyclone fence with barbed wire on top all around the base. We found a hole in the fence and went to town (Norfolk). We

got drunk and decided to get tattoos so everyone would know we went on liberty. We came back Sunday late in the day and came through the main gate and flashed a card that looked like a liberty card, really quick, to the marines guarding the base and kept on moving. They weren't that thorough when you were coming into the base.

Monday morning at muster it was obvious that the four of us were off base because of our tatoos. Everyone else was sent on work details but Clemensen, Dureau, Reed, and me. We were to wait in the warehouse in back until Lieutenant Marshall could see us. After about fifteen minutes of waiting, I decided to go to the office and see Lieutenant Marshall. He and Lieutenant Anderson were in the office talking.

Lieutenant Marshall said, "Togna, wait in the warehouse."

I said, "I have to speak to you first. It was my fault that we went off base this weekend. I talked the others into going with me."

"I don't care! They are grown men," Lieutenant Marshall said.

"That's the point, sir!" I said. "You are treating all of us like we are in the third grade. Half of us were not on base when the gun disappeared! Why punish all of us?"

Lieutenant Anderson said, "We thought someone might tell."

"You ought to know no one is going to tell you if they did know. You are training us how to do reconnaissance. Well! We should be congratulated for not getting caught by the marine guards and sentries." (At that time everything was guarded. You could not wander anywhere you wanted to on base.)

Lieutenant Marshall said, "I'll speak to you later in the warehouse, Togna!"

I went back to the warehouse and the guys wanted to know what had happened. I said, "Nothing happened." I wasn't smiling. We were putting a few things back in their places and tidying the area.

About a half hour later Lieutenant Anderson came around and said, "Go out and find your work detail and forget this ever happened."

That weekend the restriction was lifted. We never did know what happened to the gun. If they knew in the office, we were never told.

The rest of the summer we went on demos it seemed like everywhere! Some for Commander Fane. Most of the operations were like eight to eighteen men. The times we went on the Persian Gulf cruise and Newfoundland trip were about the only times the whole team went together. I would volunteer for every project that came down the pike. If I just got back from a detail, I would ask to be sent with the next group getting ready to leave for a maneuver somewhere.

Lieutenant Anderson and Lieutenant Marshall were after me again to take the test for third-class petty officer. I said, "I'm not going to. I'm getting out in a few months." (This was the summer of 1949.)

I don't know whose idea it was, but we went out one night off of Little Creek Beach about a half a mile out. We were told we were going to capture Little Creek. There were about twenty of us. A plan was set before us and this was how it played out. We swam in as if we were on a reconnaissance mission. We were to capture Little Creek from the marines who guarded the base and render the base immobile from 2200 to 2400 hours, then give the command back to the marines and retreat back to

the beach and report in. While we were in charge we were to take inventory of things and happenings going on in that period of time. We had three- and four-man groups to go to different places. One group went to the marines' barracks and secured it. Another went to the motor pool and took the keys from the jeeps so they could not run. Then another group went to the commodore's residence and informed him of the goings-on. I was with the group that went to the main gate (three of us). We had swim trunks on and our knives strapped to our sides and black grease all over our bodies.

The marines knew who we were but did not believe that we wanted to stop the cars from coming in and going out of the base. A group finally got to the electrical station and turned the electric power off. Our marines finally believed us. The cars were stopped, and we waited two hours. The lights came back on; the operation was over. Now we had to get back to the beach before the marines realized that they were just made to look foolish. Everyone got back to the beach.

Well, Commander Fane caught hell the next day from the commodore. The commodore said, "If your men have idle time on their hands, I'll keep you busy." The marines gave us a hard time for a few weeks and that was the end of it.

It was now the end of September 1949 and the team was getting ready to go to Newfoundland again. Lieutenant Anderson had a list of things he wanted me to pack and look after.

I said to Lieutenant Anderson, "I'm not going on this trip."

Lieutenant Anderson said, "No one is staying back here. Everyone in the team is going to Newfoundland."

I said, "I get discharged in November."

Lieutenant Anderson said, "We will be back by then."

I said that we were never back before Thanksgiving and "I understand you have a bigger program on this trip than ever before."

Lieutenant Anderson couldn't believe that I wasn't going and I wanted to be discharged. He actually had tears in his eyes. He said, "Togna, if anyone is a twenty-year man, you are. Lieutenant Marshall and I are trying to help you to advance by insisting you take a test for the next rate. Lieutenant Marshall and I put your name and a few others in UDT Four on a list recommended for officers candidate school. You have to be at least a third-class petty officer, which we know you will earn on this trip."

"I'm not going," I said.

"The navy will pay you if you go over your enlistment time," he said. Lieutenant Anderson went on, "You never complained; you always had a smile on your face; you seemed so happy; you were always first for anything, easy or hard. You were always there. Togna, we need you on this trip. You will come back with a third-class boatswain mate rate."

"No, thank you," I said. "I'll stay with Team Two until I get discharged."

Lieutenant Anderson said, "Commander Fane won't have you; you know that."

For the next couple of days it was the same thing. Cook and Mac were also on me to ship over. Lieutenant Anderson was really down in the mouth. He looked sad. Every time I would see him he just shrugged.

About a week before they were to ship out for New-foundland, Lieutenant Anderson said one morning, "Togna, pack your gear tomorrow. You are going to the Norfolk Naval Station for discharge."

215

I arrived at the Norfolk naval base at about 1200 hours. They were coming in to be discharged by the dozen. The base wasn't ready for this many men. There wasn't any room for men who came that day. (It was about the first week in October 1949.) There was a section at the base where a dozen or so barracks were boarded up. A few of us pulled the boards off the door and went inside, knocked the boards off the windows, found the fuse box, got ourselves light, and turned the water on. The place was dirty. There were bunks and mattresses; we settled in for the night. The next day we got heat and hot water, and then we cleaned the barracks up.

We went to the discharge office; it was mobbed. They were taking the men as their enlistment dates were up. They had a lot of men whose dates had passed; they went first.

That took about a week. I went to the pier where the ship was tied up to, to say good-bye to Cook, Mac, and the others I knew. The ship left a day early. (I missed the ship!) I never felt so lonely and lowly in my life. It looked like I would be in this crummy place until Thanksgiving. My birthday is the twenty-fifth of November. It usually fell a day or so before or after Thanksgiving. The end of my enlistment was the twenty-fifth of November. We never had a calendar to look at the whole three and a half years I was in the navy. I never knew what day of the month it was, only that it was Sunday, Friday, Wednesday, or whatever. It didn't matter when we went on a detail; we worked until it was done.

I made a pest of myself at the separation office. Finally, one of the officers said to me, "Would you like to talk to a recruiting officer?"

I said, "Why not?" If I didn't talk to anyone and kept quiet, I couldn't help myself. I was going nuts doing nothing.

I was taken down a hall with rooms on both sides with officers in them trying to sign men up again. I was left in a room, waiting for a recruiter to come in. I figured if I talked to someone, I might get out sooner. Well! Who walks in but Lieutenant Iverson, my first CO of UDT Four. He wanted to know all about UDT Four, the men who were still there and what was going on. We talked all afternoon. This was where he was assigned after leaving UDT Four. His term was coming to an end, too. He was undecided on what to do. We talked so much we did not get any paperwork done. I went back to see Lieutenant Iverson the next morning. We talked some more. Lieutenant Iverson couldn't believe the confidence I had; no schooling or trade and I was willing to go out in civilian life. He offered me third class and a thousand-dollar bonus if I signed for four more years. He thought I would do better in UDT.

I said, "No deal. Lieutenant Anderson promised me third class if I went to Newfoundland with them."

Lieutenant Iverson said, "You should have made the trip and when you got back you would have been offered this deal. You probably could get a second-class petty officer out of it."

I said, "I did not want to be tempted. I want to get married and have children and be part of a family. The service is no place for a married man."

This was a Thursday, the twenty-third of October. The twenty-fifth was on a Saturday.

Lieutenant Anderson said, "Come back tomorrow, I'll give you your discharge. We will date it the twenty-seventh, Monday. We are not supposed to let you go before your expiration date."

I said, "My expiration date is November twenty-fifth."

"We are so busy no one will pick that up."

I went back the next morning, Friday, after breakfast. Lieutenant Iverson gave me my discharge papers plus back pay and I don't remember how much traveling money in cash and a $100 check, mustering out pay, and said, "Good luck, Togna. I'm glad we had this talk. I'm going to try the outside, too."

I said good luck to Lieutenant Iverson, too. If the navy had known that I had an influence on his decision to leave the navy, I would have been put before the firing squad. Ha!

I was home only a couple of days and every farmer in the area stopped by our home and wanted to hire me. I said no to all of them. I wasn't going to work on a farm for a living. I enjoyed the work and the outdoors. There was less money per month than I was getting in the navy. I went to work for a logger and sawmill outfit that winter. All cutting was with an ax or two-man saw. Chain saws were not around at that time, the winter of 1949–50.

Now that I am done with my naval experiences, I sit here at my desk wondering if I would have ended up in UDT had I just gone with the program, the way things were going to be, take orders and just did what I was told, like when I went to New York City to enlist and after we were sworn in. The men were given two weeks to go home and wait for the navy to call us back. If I went home then, when I came back I would have ended up in the Great Lakes for my boot camp. Next time things could have changed. When I got to Little Creek after boot camp, I missed two or three callings of my name to be sent somewhere other than where I ended up. "Next time." After I got aboard the *New Kent,* I did not work so hard to get off. As I look back, my whole life was like that. I thought I was promoting myself. I don't know if I did or

not. When I didn't like the situation I was in, I became convinced of the fact that I had to do something to change it to my liking. I always made the best of a situation. I still wonder.

This is the end of my story about my hitch in the navy and UDT. A lot more incidents happened that were what you would call one-line, dull stories to get to the punch line. I don't want to let go. As Clemensen said, "Togna, leave it be." God! I enjoyed those days. Thank you for letting me relive my youth.

Part III

I Finally Made It—Tough All the Way

28

My Life from 1950 to 2000

I was discharged October 27, 1949, from UDT Four. I went home to where my parents were now living. The house had a 500-pound safe in it; you could not lock it. The people who lived there before had left it. Tony said, "It is good in case of a fire; that's all." I came home from the service with $400. I put it in the safe.

Tony was trying to go farming on his own and was inquiring about renting one of the many farms that were abandoned after the war was over. There was a cattle dealer who was the brother of Mr. Blank. He was trying to get a small herd of about thirty head of cows for Tony. Tony was clever; he thought if he had a farm all his boys would come home and work the farm. I told Tony I was not farming. Tony said he always wanted to own his own farm. I said, "Good, I'll help you get one." Tony didn't have five dollars saved. We went to all the abandoned farms and picked one that was for sale at a reasonable price and the people were willing to wait for their money.

Fred Blank got the bank to advance the money to buy the cattle with nothing down. The farm had machinery on it, Tony could use it but had to repair it first and keep it in working order.

In between working and trying to see if I could get some kind of schooling from the Veterans Administration, I would go over to the farm Tony was renting and

repair the machinery, barn, and tenant house, getting things in working order.

I had a chance to buy a 1937 Ford rumble-seat car. I brought the man home to get the $300 he wanted for the car. I went into the safe and there was only $280 there. I said to Mom, "Do you know what happened to the hundred and twenty that is missing?" Maggie said that Tony used some. I told the man, "I'll have the balance next week."

He said, "I'll take the two-eighty and call it a deal."

Tony paid me back; every time he gave me twenty dollars Tony would say, "I saved you twenty dollars."

That winter of 1949–50 I worked for a logging outfit. They were due to shut down in the spring. I was looking for work other than farm work. I could not find a job anywhere. One day I decided to go to the VA in Newburgh, New York, to see what they had to offer. After a couple of trips and a few aptitude tests it seemed that I had a great ability in the mechanical field. There was a diesel mechanic school in New York City that I could go to. That was the only school available, and it's funny that I had this mechanical ability.

My sister was living in New York City with some friends of Mrs. Stern, going to a beautician school. We had cousins who lived in Brooklyn that Lina visited once in a while. Cousin Kate mentioned to Lina that they had a spare bedroom that I could use if I decided to go to school in New York City.

This was in March of 1950. The next class was to start in April. The VA didn't think they could get the paperwork to the school in time. Everything was all set to go on my end; we just had to wait. I took a bus trip to Brooklyn to see Kate. It was agreed I would give her all the money that the VA was giving me for my room and

board while going to school. The VA paid for the school, too. Kate said, "No!"

I said, "I won't need it. I'm going to study; I won't be going anywhere."

The class started the first week in April and I was in it. There were about eighty young men in the class, eight teachers, and two people in the main office. We were broken up into ten students per teacher and every two weeks they would rotate the teachers.

School was going along great. I was getting on well with my second cousin Kate and her family. After a few weeks there was a knitting mill operation a block away that wanted night help. I went over one night after supper and got a job running a milling machine. The factory was in an old building, the loft a real fire trap. I worked four hours a night for $1.50 per hour. I had spending money now. Instead of Kate giving me a couple of dollars for the movies, I managed to give Kate a few more dollars.

After about six weeks a bulletin was posted on the board at school. The Greyhound Bus Company wanted six men from the school to go to their school to learn about the diesel engines in their buses. All their buses had the gray marine diesel in them and still do today. They did not want us until October; after we graduated we would be sent to a big city somewhere in the United States. I was one that said I would go anywhere. Well, it seemed like I was going to be a diesel mechanic somewhere.

In the late 1940s the United States was continuing the war on communism in the States. It was the first week in June we came to school and it was closed and padlocked. The school was closed indefinitely. Not only were all the teachers card-carrying communists; they also used the school for their meetings.

One of the six students who was on the list with our names on it to go to the Greyhound Bus Company knew someone at the company and told him of our dilemma. The company did not want us until October, and we had to have the six months' training from a diesel school before they could consider sending us to their school. The end of my diesel career. They closed the school. Kate was disappointed; she liked the extra money.

I went back home to the farm. The cows did not come yet; Tony was living on his farm with no cows. They were supposed to be there in May. I went to see Mr. Fred Blank; he said that he had a herd of cows coming from Canada. The farmer who owned the cows was killed and the herd was producing enough milk to make a living with. A bull was with the deal. He said they should be here within the week.

I heard they were hiring men in Neversink, New York. It was forty-five miles over the Shawangunk Mountain from home. I was told by a few people in town that I would not get hired.

I said, "I understand they need help."

"Yes, but they won't hire Italians or Catholics." Most of the men are lighter, Scandinavians, Danes, or Norwegians."

When I got there the men were all fair-headed and blue eyed. Shit! My hair was blond and I had blue eyes. I passed myself off as a Dane. Clemensen, whom I was in UDT Four with, was Danish. I remembered a few things he had said and customs. Used *Henry* and pronounced *Togna* hard and sharp. I got hired. As we worked, they would tell Italian jokes and I would tell a few, too. They admired the pleasure I got out of the jokes. I laughed loud and long and it was funny. They didn't know how funny.

The cows finally came and Tony was happy. I went to work over the mountains, and Tony went to work in the barn. I would help with the evening milking and other chores.

The next Sunday Mike came to visit. I hadn't seen him for a couple of weeks. Mike said to me, "You want everything, don't you?"

I said, "What in the hell are you talking about?"

Mike said he would come home and work with Tony.

I said, "Sure. Tony will be happy."

Mike came home and worked with Tony.

They were finishing up the outside work at the water works for the year. It was around the first of November, and the weather was getting too cold to do mason work. I got a job working in the tunnel as a chuck tender, helping the driller drill two-inch diameter holes ten to fifteen feet deep so they could be packed with dynamite to blast a hole through the mountain. The tunnel was a half-mile deep to connect two reservoirs that helped supply water to New York City. When I started to work in the tunnel, I helped Tony and Mike on Saturday and Sunday only.

I had an invitation for MacAllister's wedding in Philadelphia, September 19th (?), 1950. I had planned on going to the wedding. Mac was still in UDT, and I was sure there would be at least a half-dozen guys I knew from UDT Four at the wedding. The weekend before Mac's wedding I was driven off the road on the way home from a night out by a tractor and trailer. I cut a telephone pole off about a foot from the ground with my 1937 Ford, and I hit the pole dead center with my car and dropped a transformer and wires all around the car. A wire lying over the hood was shooting sparks all over the place. I kicked open the door and jumped free of the car, not touching the ground and car at the same time. This was

after 2:00 A.M. I was about three miles from home, so I walked home. When I came in the house Tony was up and said, "Somebody must have hit an electric pole; there are no electric lights. We will have to milk by hand; how about you helping us milk?" I had been out drinking, so it was a while, about halfway through milking, before I realized I was the one who hit the electric pole. Mike said, "You have a bump on your nose," and now it started to hurt. By the time we got all the work done and into the house for breakfast the power was on.

I noticed Maggie was getting a big belly. I said to her, "Are you pregnant?"

Maggie said, "No." Sometimes she would go on an eating binge.

A few days later I asked her again. She insisted she was not pregnant. She said it was a tumor. I said, "Get into the car; I'm taking you to Dr. Boutzell. The way that tumor is growing, it's going to be bigger than you in a couple of weeks." We saw Boutzell. After examining Maggie, he came out of his office and said, "Henry, your mother is pregnant. Take her to Dr. Dewitt downtown. I'll call him and tell him you are coming."

Dr. Dewitt confirmed that Maggie was pregnant. I asked him what I owed him. He said nothing. I said, "Thank you."

A few months later, Maggie was ready to give birth. Tony told Mike that a few hours after Maggie lost her water the baby would be born. Maggie had lost her water that morning. Mike put Mom in the car and raced to Kingston, about thirty miles north of home. All the other children Maggie had were born at home (other than Tony, Jr.) with the help of a midwife. Mike got to the hospital, and they told him it's a false alarm; it will be a couple more days.

Mike said, "You keep her here. I'm not going through that again. Her water broke; she should be having the baby soon." Mike left Maggie at the hospital and came home.

When I came home from work and heard the news, I made a call. I don't remember what was going around at that time, a virus of some kind. They didn't want visitors at the hospital. One of us went to a neighbor every night and called to hear about Maggie's progress. Maggie was there six days before Frances was born. I went to Kingston to see Maggie in the hospital. I went to the maternity ward.

The nurse said, "Only the father or husband of the patient is allowed in to visit. Are you the husband?"

I said, "Yes."

"Let me see your driver's license."

The name was the same. I was in my work clothes and had five days' growth of beard. I said, "I want to see my baby girl."

As I walked to see Maggie, the nurses were whispering in the hall and looking at me. While I was in the room with Maggie five or six nurses came into the room to check on Maggie or the other women in the room. Later they showed me Frances, my kid sister. She was a very pretty baby. I asked when Maggie would come home. The day and time were written down for me. As I was leaving there were six or seven nurses around the desk making like they were doing something. I said, "Good night. I will see you in a couple of days to pick up my mother and my baby sister; take good care of them." I heard them laughing until I left the building.

I was using Mike's car, waiting for a loan to be approved by the bank. I was buying a new 1951 Kaiser. My Ford was totaled when I hit the pole. (I never did get to

Mac's wedding.) My car was at the dealer's just waiting for me. The dealer finally called me and said, "Hank, the loan is approved. They want you to pick up the check personally. I don't know why."

I said, "You are going to have to wait until Saturday, and I'll see if Mike can take me."

The dealer said he would pick me up and after I gave him the check I could have the car. He would get the license plates and have it ready to roll.

Mike and I went to the bank on Saturday morning to get the money. The woman at the bank said to come into her office. We talked a few minutes; she asked what I did before I went into the navy and about my hitch in the navy and what my plans for the future were.

As the conversation died down, I asked, "Why didn't you send the check to the dealer after the loan was approved? Isn't that what is usually done?"

She said, "Yes, I just couldn't believe the references! Everyone I called said, 'Give the kid whatever he wants,' and each one gave me another name to call if I wanted to. I did! I called everybody! Do you know there are people out there that I talked to who are waiting in line to sign for you if need be?"

I smiled and said, "Great!"

She said, "You're not twenty-two years old! It usually takes a man thirty-five or forty years to achieve that kind of status and trust these people have in you. I just had to meet you; that's all. I've been doing this for years and no one this young has ever had this kind of reputation."

Early in December, one morning when we arrived for work at the tunnel to start our shift we were told the job was shut down indefinitely. The tunnel was full of water. The last shift when they blasted, the work area, which was under a big lake, opened up the cracks in the

stone we were blasting through. The lake drained into the tunnel. It looked like a couple of months before they would get the water out of the tunnel and stop the leaks. We were given our pay and left a phone number to get in touch.

We went to Grandpa's for Christmas (1950) dinner. We had to leave early to get back to the farm and milk. Uncle Nick was a bricklayer working out of the union hall. He asked me if I wanted to learn the mason trade. He had an opportunity to work on his own if I would come to Newark, New Jersey, and work as his helper. He would teach me the mason trade. We would eventually become partners. Sounded good. Tony and Mike was all the help needed on the farm. There wasn't enough money coming in for two, after paying the loan and feed bill.

I moved to my Uncle Nick's in January (1951). I worked as a laborer for Nick. After I had him set up, I would grab a trowel and help him with the brickwork or stonework, whatever kind of mason work we were doing. I was a fast learner. I had the knack of seeing something done and I'd do it with ease. Nick was surprised at how fast I learned things and how I would improve as we worked.

I would go home about once a month to see Tony, Mike, Maggie, and baby Frances. I would buy tobacco and a bottle of booze for Tony. Maggie liked chocolate, and a few bottles of baby food, and Mike, I would give a twenty-dollar bill so he could go out on a Saturday night. They were not making enough money for any pleasures.

Maggie was neglecting baby Frances and the men, too. Maggie would not do anything, cook or clean or feed the baby. Here it was again, postpartum depression. Of course, when we were younger we didn't know what was going on. Now Mike and Lina understood a little why

Maggie behaved so. I was able to forgive Mom and realized she had a problem. (I felt bad.)

Tony wanted me to go and get Helen from Mrs. White, just like that. Helen's name was never mentioned by my father all the time we were growing up. Helen could be useful now. Helen was about fourteen years old. Can you imagine, bringing a kid to a home like this? Helen didn't even know we existed. Tony and I had our first real argument. I told him I would not get that girl to bring her into this mess; that would be a terrible thing to do. We went at each other for over an hour. Mike said for us to stop. We were saying some nasty things to each other. I left and I told Mike, "Don't you go and try to get Helen."

I could not wait a whole month. Two weeks went by. I went home on a Friday night. Frances was gone. Maggie didn't respond to my conversation, and it seemed Maggie didn't recognize me or acknowledge that I was there talking to her. It was like talking to a zombie. I asked Mike what had happened. The landlord was moving out of the main house to live with her daughter. She was about six months beyond the time that she promised to give Tony the main house. Mrs. Sisto's daughter saw the condition of baby Frances and offered to take her for a while. They just moved into a new house near Newburgh. Tony and I got into it again. I said, "You don't know how lucky you are to have people like that around to help."

Mike told me he took Tony to see Helen. I was mad and said, "What the hell is the matter with you?!" Mike said Tony kept on all day, half the night, for us to see Helen. I finally gave in. We went to the school in Vails Gate where Tony said Helen was in sixth or seventh grade. Tony went to the principal of the school and asked to see a girl about fourteen years old by the name of Helen

Togna. Tony, standing there in his work clothes, with four or five days' growth of beard, badly in need of a haircut, looked like a bum. The principal said, "No." Tony then asked if a girl by the name of Helen White was in school? The principal said "Yes." The principal listened to Tony and sent for the girl. (This part of the story was told to me about five years later by Helen.)

Helen entered the principal's office and was introduced to her father, Tony. Helen at first thought it was a joke! Helen had never before heard the name Togna. The principal was telling her it was true. I don't know what the principal knew; with gossip and all the shenanigans going on in their house, what gave him the right to do that to Helen? (Educated people.) Tony never went to see Mrs. White. Helen left the school crying and went home to confront her mother. At that time Mrs. White told Helen who she was. Mrs. White had relatives in Connecticut. The next day they sent Helen there to live and finish the school year. Tony never did try to see Mrs. White or Helen again. The story Helen tells is that Mrs. White could not have any children. Her father-in-law would not leave any money to his son in his will until they had a baby. So this opportunity was just right for Mrs. White.

I stayed away from home for a few months. I was living with my Uncle Nick. He and his wife, Terry, would go out every Friday night to a Chinese restaurant, and they would always ask me to come along. I said, "No."

"Who not?"

"Because they serve cat meat in their food."

"They do not," Aunt Terry said.

"I don't like Chinese food," I would say. I would grab something to eat somewhere and I would go hang out at

the YMCA in Newark and go to a dance now and then at the Y.

It was wintertime in early February when the garbagemen were picking up the garbage at Captain Joe's Famous Chinese restaurant, the one Terry loved best of all. One of the men slipped on the ice, emptying the garbage can, spilling the contents all over the parking lot, cat heads, cat skins, cat intestines. There were over twenty garbage cans full of animal parts. The city of Newark closed the restaurant. My Aunt Terry, when she read it in the papers, went to the bathroom and heaved her guts out. Every time she saw me she would cuss me for letting her go to that restaurant when "I knew!" they served cat, rat, and dog, according to the newspapers. I reminded Terry she had eaten at that restaurant for many years before I came to Newark. Terry ran to the bathroom again; she could not keep any food in her stomach. She puked for weeks; she lost forty pounds and learned a few more cusswords to use on me. Later she asked how I knew they served cat and dog meat in the restaurant. I said I did not know. A kid from Boston, while I was in the navy, told us a story about a famous Chinese restaurant that was closed by the city for serving cat, rat, and dog meat. I said, "If you read your history, the Chinese raise dogs and rats to eat in China."

One night I got all spruced up and went to the YMCA for a dance. There was no dance that night; somehow I got the date wrong. Across the street was an Arthur Murray dance studio. The windows were open, and I could hear the music. I listened for a while and decided to see what was going on. I signed up for ten one-hour lessons for sixty dollars. It was an introductory course. I wasn't doing well at the dances at the Y. I figured it would help. After a couple of lessons I saw this one teacher I would

like to know better. Her name was Bette Mack. The next time I went for a lesson I asked Bette Mack if I could take her home when they quit for the night. They worked until 10:00 P.M. Bette said, "Teachers can't go out with the students; it's a rule here at the studio."

"I'll see you outside; they can't tell you how to live your life away from the studio."

Bette said, "No, I have a date."

I became friendly with a few male teachers and I went out with them to the bars after the studio closed. I inquired about Bette Mack. George and Joe started to laugh. I said, "What's so funny?"

"Of all the girls in the place, you picked the one that won't go out with anyone. If you want to make out, any of the other girls would be glad to go out with you."

I had one more lesson to finish my course. I was given a different teacher every time I came to the studio. They were trying to sign me up for more classes. Each girl tried to get me to take them out. I played dumb, and partly because I was shy (yeah, hard to believe).

Bette never did teach me at the studio. I did not see her there that night. I was waiting for George to go out with after he finished with his female student. George was trying to sell her more lessons and went over the time. It was about 11:00 P.M. when we went to leave the studio. It was raining outside and Bette Mack was waiting for the rain to let up before she would walk about five blocks to Springfield Avenue to catch a bus to Maplewood, where she lived. I asked Bette to let me take her home.

She said, "No."

I said, "George will come with us, won't you George? You know George."

George said, "Come on, Bette; let us take you home."

Bette said, "OK."

This one teacher was trying to sell me more lessons and after each lesson that was supposed to be my last lesson, I had one more hour coming to me. If she was not with a student we would dance a little. If she had a student, my time was listed as a no-show. She was actually trying to get me to date her. She was interested in me for herself rather than selling me lessons. In the meantime I was trying to date Bette. After several attempts I got to take her home and then to a movie, then home. This girl was naive and basically an honest and a very, very serious girl. I was partially naive and shy.

One night when I took Bette home from the studio I asked if she was going to invite me in to meet her family and have coffee. Bette said, "We don't have any coffee in the house."

I said, "I don't believe it." Bette drank coffee every chance she could.

The next time I brought her home I said, "You will have to invite me in tonight; I have a pound of coffee in the glove compartment."

When we got to her house we were standing at the front door and Bette said, "Where is the coffee?"

I said, "You've got to be kidding. You really thought I had coffee with me?" I saw a worried look come over her.

Bette was real nervous and edgy as her kid sister, Joan, opened the door. Bette's mother had the coffee on. I said, "It seems someone bought coffee for me."

I stopped in for coffee at Bette's house quite often after that night. Bette's father was a tyrant with his family and did not approve of the previous boys she brought home. He would always shame her or embarrass the boy. It was a couple of weeks before Bette felt at ease with me in the house in front of her father. It seemed that I was getting along with him.

It was now sometime in August. I was going to New York to visit Tony, Maggie, and Mike on the farm about once a month. One weekend I asked Bette if she would like to go with me to the country. Bette wasn't sure if she could go. I said, "If you are not going, I will leave Friday night and stay for the weekend."

Bette said, "I can't go for the weekend!"

I said, "I didn't expect you to. If you go, we will go either Saturday or Sunday, whatever day would be good for you."

On the way upstate to my home on Sunday to visit my parents with Bette, we were talking and Bette asked, "What does this mean, me going up to see your mother and father?"

I said, "Before we date too long I thought you should see where I came from and from whom, that's all."

Bette said, "I mean you haven't kissed me or tried to. I don't know what to think."

I said, "If you would sit closer to me I'll kiss you, if that's what's bothering you." (I'm a real lover boy, aren't I?)

When I got to the farm just Tony and Maggie were there. Mike was living with his girlfriend and had gotten a job trucking the farmer's milk to the creamery every morning. Mike would see Tony every morning at pickup time, and later that day if Tony needed help Mike would come by and help.

Bette met Tony and Maggie that Sunday. We visited awhile, Maggie made something to eat. She seemed to be in good spirits that Sunday. We were standing outside in the front of the house and I said to Tony, "I see a wood-chuck in the middle of the hay field that you and Mike just hayed." Tony said to shoot it; he couldn't see as good as he used to. I went inside and got my .22-caliber rifle.

I put the rifle on top of a fence post; the woodchuck was about two hundred yards away in the middle of a ten-acre hay field. I shot. Tony asked if I got it?

I said, "I don't know; I did not see it fall. It might have slipped back into its hole before I shot."

Bette was standing there; she didn't see anything. Bette thought I was shooting at air.

Tony said, "Go see if you got it."

Bette said, "Yeah, Hank, I'd like to see what a wood-chuck looks like."

I went to the woodchuck hole and there it was sitting up in the hole, dead. I brought it back to show Bette, and Tony wanted it for meat. We were talking. Tony took out his penknife and tied the woodchuck to a fence post with some baling twine and skinned the woodchuck and cleaned it up.

Bette was looking at Tony, then at me, making all kinds of facial expressions. I thought at one point Bette was going to get sick to her stomach. Tony put the wood-chuck into the oven.

Bette said, "It's not even cold yet!"

I said, "We save on kerosene. What's the difference? The oven is going to be over three hundred degrees in a little while."

Bette looked at me, bewildered.

I said, "You don't have to eat it." At that point I realized I made a big mistake bringing Bette to meet my parents. They looked like real hillbillies, and I had to put the icing on the cake by shooting an animal in front of her. This city girl felt bad when you killed a mouse or rat in the city and Bette knew if you didn't they would take over.

I figured on the way home to Maplewood that night I would hear a lot of excuses why we should take our

time on thinking about anything serious. Nothing was said on the way home about my folks or the shooting. When we got to Maplewood I kissed Bette good night. She did not resist. I figured maybe I still had a chance. Bette let me kiss her a second time. I saw her about once a week the next couple of months.

The next time I went home, I went alone for the weekend. Baby Frances was home with Maggie and Tony. I asked what happened. Tony said one day the Sistos came to the house with adoption papers for him to sign. Tony said, "Nothing doing," and told them to bring the baby back to him.

Lina came back to Mrs. Stern's from NYC and found work as a beautician in a beauty shop in New Paltz.

I was working with Uncle Nick; we were doing brickwork and stonework, sometimes a section of sidewalk. Sometimes Nick wouldn't have any work to do because he only knew how to do brick, stone, and sidewalks. I would say to Nick, "Block work or footings and cement floors are just as easy to do as the other work. You just have to work a little harder and faster doing it; that's all." We were working for a builder for whom Nick and I did just the brickfronts of the houses. The masonry contractor they had doing the foundations was busy elsewhere. The carpenter was worried that by the time he finished framing the house the other foundation would not be ready for him. I said to Nick, "Let's us do the foundation." Nick was afraid to. I went and talked to Harry and Jimmy. Long story short: we started to do the foundations for them. We were busy and now we had to work on Saturdays, too. Nick didn't like that. We had trouble getting help. On one of my trips to New York to see Tony and Maggie, Mike was home helping Tony fix

the barn roof. I helped them finish the job. Mike was looking for work; the milk trucking job did not pan out.

Nick and Terry had a baby early that spring; I had to move out. I rented a room in the city of Orange, New Jersey. It was a half hour to work, to Bette's house, and to Nick's. I brought Mike to New Jersey to work with us.

Bette and I decided we would like to be married. Bette was worried that her father would not approve of our being married. We agreed that I would ask her father for permission to get married and if Mr. McCluskey, Bette's father, said no, Bette and I would marry anyway, and I would tell him so! One night when all of Bette's family were home and we were having coffee and cake. I told or asked them my intentions. Everyone was happy and wished us well. That night we set the date of the wedding, November 16, 1952.

Mike went home every weekend to see his girl, Marie, and would be back by Monday for work. This Monday he did not show; we had to work without him. When I came home from work he was not there, nor was there a message. Nick thought I knew Mike had quit. That next weekend I went home and looked up Mike's girl. Marie said her brother had a good deal for him and Mike, painting up old masonry buildings with some contractor in Albany, New York for four dollars per hour. They had to be there Monday morning first thing to get hired, Marie said. Mike said I would be around to see what happened.

Bette came along for the ride. We stopped at the farm to see Tony and Maggie and baby Frances. Frances was out in the barn with Tony; she was just over two years old. Frances would not talk; she was very shy. Bette tried to get Frances to talk for over an hour. She wouldn't shake her head yes or no, either, just stood there looking back at you with a facial expression like, "What's the

problem?" Tony was done milking and was letting the cows out of the barn. As the cows go outside the barn they always have a bowel movement and mess up the barn floor, so you have to clean up. Well, I thought Bette was going to have a bowel movement! Little Frances, with a stick in her hand, was hollering, "Tony! Tony! The sons of bitches are shitting all over the place!" Frances was hollering this over and over as she drove the cows out of the barn. I started to laugh! Bette was floored! She said, "Hank, Frances can talk!" It brought instant recall back to me, when I was always with my father on the farm in Avon, Connecticut. I was about three years old. Boy, did things come back into focus for a few seconds. Bette took a few minutes to say, "Hank, something has to be done about her language." Yea.

Mike was to be best man in my wedding in November. I wanted to see him and Tony, Jr., about coming to Jersey to be fitted for the tux around the end of October. Tony, Jr. told me Mike was in the hospital in Kingston, New York. After working in Albany for a couple of weeks Mike took sick and was admitted to a hospital.

Bette and I went to see Mike. He was bedridden and being treated for bulbar polio. Mike couldn't sit up in bed. So it was agreed Tony, Jr., would be best man. Clifford Dureau, who was in UDT Four with me, was coming to my wedding as a guest. I called him to ask if he would be an usher. Dureau accepted!

Before we married on November 16, 1952, it was agreed that Bette and I would spend the winter in Florida. There was no work of the kind my Uncle Nick did in cold weather. It would be too expensive to provide heat for the mason work to be done in the winter, so the work stopped until spring.

Bette and I saved enough money for our wedding. I had fifty dollars left after paying the bill. The money we collected after the wedding and counted was twenty dollars more than the hotel bill. It was just over $500.

Marie, Mike's girl, came late to the wedding. She told us the doctors wanted Mike in a New York City cancer hospital. They finally diagnosed that Mike had Hodgkin's disease and they could treat him better in NYC. Marie had just come from the hospital after going to Kingston early that morning and bringing Mike to NYC by herself. The first day of our marriage Bette and I were in a New York City hospital trying to find my brother to see him. Was he glad to see us!! They would not take any test or give him treatment needed to relieve his discomfort. I signed a number of papers approving of any and all tests that Mike would have to undergo.

The twentieth of November 1952, we finally got to Newport News and took the ferry ride to Norfolk. A few minutes later we were in Little Creek. Everybody I knew in UDT Four was glad to see us. The base was still the same as it was when I left in 1949. Cook invited us to his house for supper. He and his wife gave up their bedroom for us and took the spare room. They would not have it any other way. The next morning I found out they slept on the floor on some blankets. McAllister and DiMartino and their wives came over to Cook's house that evening. We had a wonderful time talking about old times.

When Bette and I left Norfolk it was raining heavy. We stopped at a motel outside of Elizabeth City, North Carolina. We had supper in town, then went to a movie. On our way back to the motel, at an intersection, a car coming very fast hit us on the left side and turned us completed around, knocking the trunk open to spill some

of our luggage. I received a cut on the hairline of my head. The police took me to a hospital where I received six stitches. The car was towed to a Kaiser-Frazer dealer. The next week we spent in Elizabeth City, North Carolina, trying to make a deal with the Kaiser-Frazer dealer to trade our car for a Kaiser deluxe model. He was trying to take advantage of me in our predicament. The dealer had my car locked up in his garage every night. After a couple of days I told him, "No deal." He had the idea or notion that we were running away from our rich parents. I finally had it. I broke into his garage one night, I wired the door shut and stuffed a couple of blankets in the opening around the door, and drove out. For the next couple of days Bette got jumpy every time we saw a police car.

We just kept driving south on Route 1. That was the only major road that went south at that time. When we got into Florida I just kept driving south to Miami. We passed through Miami to Kendall. It was about 4:00 P.M. I stopped at a gas station and asked the man if anyone in that area had rooms to rent for six months. He said, "Mrs. Zidrich, one mile down Route One. Turn left onto a dirt road; go until you see a house on the right she has for rentals." We rented one side of a small duplex with a kitchen, bath, living room, and bedroom.

That night as we settled in, Bette came to the realization that she must be crazy. Then Bette said, "I'm not crazy; you are!"

I said, "Take it easy." Our money was very low. I said, "I'll go and look for work tomorrow."

Bette said, "What are you going to do?" I said, "Anything." I had all the confidence in the world that I would find some kind of work to do. I didn't care what it was; I would do it if it paid American dollars.

Next morning I went back to the gas station and asked the man at the station, Jake, "Is there any work in the area?" Jake asked what I could do? I said, "Mason or carpentry work, but I'll do anything, you name it and I'll do it."

Jake said, "Come back in the morning. I know Bill is looking for a mason. You can do mason work, right?"

I said, "Yes."

"We will know by tomorrow night."

I worked for Bill until the middle of February. Our landlady was remodeling her home. It needed a lot of work. She asked me if I would work for her. We agreed on a price per hour, and she would keep a record and deduct what I earned from the rent. I didn't pay any more rent the rest of the time I was there. I would pick up a side job for cash.

Bette was getting homesick and wanted to go home. I said as soon as I finished what I started for the landlady and got $200 in cash we would go home. It was near the end of May that we packed up and came home to New Jersey.

We pulled up to a light two blocks from Bette's home, and her two sisters were standing, waiting for the light to change, on their way to church. They went to a later mass that Sunday. We stayed at Bette's parents' home for a week until we rented a one-room studio apartment, which had a tiny kitchen and a bathroom. It was about fifteen minutes away from Bette's parents'. I got a job with a builder working in the area. This was in the second week in June 1953.

A few days after the Fourth of July my uncle Nick found the job I was working on. I was building a fireplace. Nick said, "Where did you learn to build a fireplace?"

I said, "Florida." (The contractor I worked for in Florida! I told him my uncles taught me the trade. I can do anything! I never told Nick this!)

Nick wanted me to come and work for him. He would pay me $2.50 per hour.

I said, "No! I'm getting three dollars" (which was a lie).

Nick said, "OK, I'll match it."

I said, "This man has a lot of work. He promised me work for at least a year."

Nick said, "I have work for a couple of years. I just signed three more contracts in the town of Linden for two-story all-brick duplexes."

I said, "Three-twenty-five per hour and I work all day" ($26.00 a day) "at least five days a week. I can do anything, cement, plaster, concrete work, stucco, any kind of brickwork. You name it, I can do it."

Uncle Nick agreed.

I said, "OK, but I'm finishing this fireplace and chimney for this man so he can finish this house. He has been good to me."

I started to work for Uncle Nick in the middle of July. In August Uncle Eugene came to New Jersey and started to work with us. The Friday after Labor Day, Nick paid me and said he didn't need me anymore. Uncle Eugene left early that afternoon, saying he had a doctor's appointment. I called Nick a son of a bitch for starters! I said, "You knew this a couple of weeks ago. As a matter of fact, it was a done deal when Eugene came to work with us."

Nick said, "Yes!"

I asked, "Why didn't you tell me sooner, so I would have a chance to get a job."

He said, "If I told you, then you would get a job and leave me before we finished this house."

I asked him to give me work for one more week. "I have a wife now to take care of," I said. "I don't get it. We got along great and I worked hard for you." Nick said that he had just had enough work for him and Eugene until bad weather.

I said, "What happened to the two years you promised me?"

He said, "That's all changed now."

I left work in a fog. On the way home to Maplewood I went straight through an intersection where I always turned left on to go home. I did this for weeks. I ended up turning here and there, trying to get to a main road to home. I came to an area where they were building new homes. I pulled into the little development. I walked up to the office in a trailer. Who comes to the door but Harry, a builder Nick and I worked for a year ago in Livingston? They were building twenty-one homes on this tract. They had two models up and were building a third, one of which was sold. They were looking for a mason contractor. I told them I just got laid off and was ready to go to work. We talked for a while. Harry said they were winding down for the season. I was selling myself, telling him all the things I could do. I gave him my phone number and went home. Bette was floored when I told her what had happened. I told her not to worry; this time of year I would find work because everyone was trying to get all the mason work they could done before cold weather.

We had planned on going upstate to see Tony and Maggie and Frances. Mike was living at home, all crippled and recovering slowly. He was working in a slicing machine factory. Tony, Jr., was in the army. Lina had a boyfriend and was planning a wedding. This we found

out on Sunday! I went out early Saturday morning and went to many construction sites looking for work. I didn't have any luck. When I got home it was late. Harry had called and wanted to talk to me. He left a number to call. I called and we made an appointment for the next day, Sunday.

I had to meet him in Mendham. Bette came with me, for when I got done talking to Harry we were going on to New York State. Harry was building a big house. He had fired two mason contractors, as they made many mistakes and were doing sloppy work. He wanted to know if I could correct the mistakes and fix up the bad work and finish the job. I said, "Nothing to it! I won't be able to give you a price. I don't know how much I have to take down to get started right." We agreed that I would get three dollars per hour and two dollars per hour for a helper. I said, "I'll work the first week without a helper, because I will be wrecking most of the time." Well, you don't know how happy I was; talk about fate! I can't explain things like this. Many times in my life this type of thing happened to me. I was fired on Friday and had a job to go to on Monday.

We went to see Tony and Maggie on the farm. Mike was living at home. He and is girl called off their wedding. The doctor told us Mike had about three years to live. Mike was never told this; the doctor didn't believe in telling the patient his predictions.

Mike wanted to work for me. I told him I didn't think he could do the work. Monday I went to work for Harry. I was still taking down brick on Thursday. Harry thought I was making a big deal out of destroying his house. He said, "I don't want you to take any more brickwork down."

We got into a big argument. I tried to tell him, "I still have to take some more down. The mason didn't plan for the sills or headers; the courses are wrong."

Harry said, "No more. Tomorrow I want you to start laying brick on my house."

"Another two days and I will have it to where I can work better," I said.

He said, "No."

I hired a helper and we went to work brick-veneering Harry's house. He came by every day and was happy with the progress.

After three weeks we had half the brickwork done. Harry came over to me and said, "I should have listened to you; that brickwork I stopped you from taking down looks like shit. Can you take that brickwork out of the wall?"

I said, "Not now. I would have to take down what I did on top of it."

Harry said, "I can't believe how bad it looks alongside your brickwork."

I said, "Plant a lot of shrubs there to hide it."

I had no truck to move my equipment that I had started to accumulate. I was using my car and made a couple of trips to move my stuff. I had an insurance policy with Prudential. It was a twenty-year endowment I had taken out when I was fifteen years old while working for Newkirk. If I died I didn't want Tony to have to have the burden of burying me. It was about ten years old. I wanted to cash it in to get $500 to buy an old telephone utility truck. The insurance men came to the house to give me the money on the cashed-in policy. Then they tried to get some of the money back by trying to sell me more insurance. I said, "All I want is another one-thousand-dollar endowment." They just would not listen; they kept on telling me what insurance I needed. After all, what would my wife, Bette, do if I were to die suddenly? I had it at this point. I got up from our kitchen table and

said to the two men, "Come over here," to where Bette was sitting on the sofa, bored. I said, "Look at her. She is as healthy as a horse; she will get a job!" The two men looked at each other, picked up their attaché cases and said good night. I hate it when someone tries to lay a guilt trip on me.

Harry was pleased with the work I did. His brother-in-law Jimmy was to start a big house that spring, and another brother-in-law would start one in the summer. Harry and Jimmy sold a few more houses in Hillside. I got all the mason work. My brother Mike came down to work for me. He lived with Bette and me. I taught Mike the mason trade. He started to respond well to the hard work; as a matter of fact, I think the work helped Mike to recover quicker. Mike was looking healthier by the day. Maybe Bette's cooking helped, too. Bette was and still is an excellent cook.

We would go upstate to New York about every two months to see Tony, Maggie and baby Frances. One of the trips Bette said to me that she would like to take Frances. Maggie was neglecting the kid again.

I brought this up to Tony. He said, "No, you want to take my only pleasure I have left."

I said, "Look at her. When was the last time Frances had a bath? The dirt on her ankles is stuck on to her skin at least a quarter-inch thick. She still eats with her hands, and she still does not talk."

"You can't take her," Tony said.

Lina was going to be married this summer. She went to New York City and had a complete checkup in the hospital that Mr. Stern managed. Lina was complaining about having difficulty breathing. It was discovered that Lina had a bad heart and should not have any children.

The strain on her heart of having a baby would be too much.

I was doing well in my business, working my fool head off. I had a five-man crew now. Doing the work was no problem; collecting the money was the problem. At times I literally begged for my money. The customer would use all kinds of reasons that had nothing to do with the fact that he owed me money. I said in the past I loved my freedom. I was trapped more now than ever. I became a self-disciplined workaholic. For some reason I enjoyed it! Money? Challenge? To prove I could do it? I guess.

This is as good a place as any in this story to tell what I used to say to a client or customer I was working for when he would ask where I learned the trade. At first when I told him I just started into business and worked a few years as an apprentice, I was criticized. I said I was a quick learner. I soon learned to elaborate and accredit my uncles with being very talented men for whom I worked every summer out of school and on weekend when I was needed. And they taught me everything from the footing to the roof.

That was for my customers. Now! These were my uncles' true qualifications in the building trade. Uncle Clarence was an auto mechanic and never did any construction work. Uncle Eugene drove a laundry truck for twenty-five years until he came to work for Nick. Uncle Joe made the navy his career. Uncle Nick was the only one who was in the building trades. He was a bricklayer only until I came to work for him. I pushed him into taking on other mason work. These uncles did not know how great they were in my stories. As years went on and I built a reputation and had many references. I did not have to tell these stories anymore. Talking to a customer,

him telling me what he wanted, I could envision the finished project. It was a natural ability I had. When I think back, I had many natural abilities. Thank God!

It was the winter of 1953–54, and just Mike and I were working. I could not collect money owed to me. The jobs were done more than three months ago, all the complaints were taken care of, even complaints not related to my work. There are a lot of rotten people out there. I had a number of customers who would try anything to embarrass or shame me so they would not have to pay me money owed to me. I never quit trying to collect; sometimes it would take a year. I would not lose sleep over it. I kept a "black book," and whenever it rained or there was other bad weather so we could not work, I would go out to these derelicts and beg for my money. I let them know that the only way I would stop was when I was paid in full. I would go to their houses on Sunday, Saturday night, even sometimes to a party they were giving. There was Hank in his work clothes, looking humble and begging for his money. I worked for lawyers, doctors, engineers, all people who could pay. One fellow said to me, "Aren't you ashamed of yourself?"

I said, "No. You don't know what shame is, Mister." One of these delinquents had a friend of his call me to do some work for him. When he told me who recommended me I told him I wouldn't even come over to see what he wanted done. I told him his friend was no good, he owed me over a thousand dollars, and I was having trouble collecting my money from him. Why would I work for a friend of a guy like this, so he could do the same thing? By the end of the week I got a check in the mail with an apology from this man and a note asking me to call his friend. I did, and I did the work, and he paid me.

I started to size people up and listen to more of what they said and study them a little. I tried to figure out their personalities. Rather than trying to get the job as number one, I started to weed out who I thought was no good (NG). I'm not sure that every one I tagged as NG was NG. All I know is the people that I picked to work for I got along great with. I would go for a few years with no trouble; then I would get a real "bastard." I did not fool around. I just pulled off the job until things got straightened out. Every once in a while I needed a jerk like that to remind me of all the good people out there. I became lifetime friends with some people I worked for.

February 1954, I came home from trying to collect some money. Bette was not home. I left Mike home; I had an errand to do. When I was done I stopped at my mother-in-law's to see if she knew where Bette was. Bette was there.

Bette said, "Sit down, Hank. I have some sad news to tell you."

I said, "Let's have it."

Bette just looked at me, very sad. We looked at each other eye-to-eye and I knew something awful was about to be told to me. "Your father, Tony, was killed today. He fell off the tractor."

Bette was not feeling well the last couple of weeks. She had allergies to many things. Bette was very upset. We waited until morning to go upstate to the farm. When we got there, Grandpa, Edith, Uncle Nick, Mary, Clarence, and Joe (he was home on leave from the navy) were there with Maggie and Frances.

Tony was driving the tractor a little too fast, when he hit a large stone and the jolt knocked him into the air. Maggie happened to be looking out the window at the time and saw it happen. When Tony fell to the ground

one of the big rear wheels ran over his head, crushing it. The tractor kept on going until it ran into the swamp and buried itself.

A cattle dealer was called, and we sold the cows. Tony owed a few people money. I went to some of the people who were having it tough and promised to pay what Tony owed them. The next year when I collected some money from one of my late debtors I would use this money to pay Tony's debts.

It was a sad time, and it got even more sorrowful. Grandpa and my uncles wanted me to spend whatever it took to buy the best casket, hire a limo for the family to ride in, and get a cement casket to save the wood from rot. Well, Tony always said, as far back as I could remember, if we were to find him dead somewhere on the farm, dig a hole right where he fell and bury him right there. We did a little better. It was February, cold as the north pole. The plot cost fifteen dollars and it cost thirty-five dollars to dig the hole for the grave. We all drove to the church in our own cars. After mass we carried Tony 200 feet from the church to the hole in the ground he said he wanted. Every time I went upstate, either hunting or visiting, I would stop at the grave site and say hello to Tony. He was lodging only 300 feet from the main road. Tony, Jr., his namesake, arrived the day we buried Tony, Sr., from somewhere in the Midwest. Tony, Jr., was in the army.

Grandpa took Maggie with little Frances to Mahopac with him. Everyone left after the burial. Grandpa took everything Maggie wanted. The next day we burned all the paper and clothes, cleaned out the house, burned what was junk, and left everything that was in good shape. Tony, Jr., was staying at a friend's house near there. Mike and I had to get back to New Jersey. I took

another look at what I could see of the tractor. The edge of the seat and a piece of one of the wheels was all that stuck out of the water and the ice in the swamp.

Things did not change much. I worked hard and it was still harder to get paid in those early years. We found out why Bette was sicker than usual. This was morning sickness; Bette was pregnant. Our first child was born October 8, 1954, Lina wanted to help out, so she took a week off from work and left her husband, Fred, home alone in New Paltz. Bette always said Lina was more work than help. Lina said she read in the paper that our sister Helen White was getting married in a few weeks. I said I would like to go to the wedding.

Lina said, "How? You don't have an invitation."

I said, "I mean to the church. Anyone can go to the church. When we leave we will get in line and wish the bride and groom well. I will give them an envelope with some money and a note saying who I am and if she wants to see me anytime to get in touch."

Lina wanted to go, too. When the time came, Bette and I went to New Paltz to get Fred and Lina to go to Helen's wedding. Fred said we should not go.

I said, "I am going." Lina just couldn't go against what Fred wanted. Bette and I went to the wedding. While we were in the church everyone was looking and pointing at us. Then the groom came into the church. When Helen came in you would swear the girl was Maggie. Helen looked like she was cloned from Maggie. They could have passed for twins.

When we met Helen at church I introduced myself, saying who I and my wife, Bette, were. I gave Helen the envelope. She did not hear me say, "My wife, Bette" (as we found out later). Helen looked Bette over from top to bottom and from bottom to top. (Bette is a very pretty

woman.) Helen was thinking the girl next to me was Lina. Lina managed in a beauty shop in New Paltz. (What better way to pass news on?) Everyone knew Lina was going to Helen's wedding with her brother. My wife, Bette, is a beautiful woman with a shapely body. I guess Helen just could not believe that her sister Lina, was that pretty.

Back at Lina and Fred's apartment Lina wished that she had come with us. Over eighteen years had passed since I had last seen Helen in 1936. Lina never did remember her as a baby.

Mike was recovering from Hodgkin's; he looked great and looked as healthy as a horse. He accidentally ran into his old girlfriend; they started to court and got married that year. Marie got a job as a secretary to an insurance company nearby.

Later that year Lina informed us she was pregnant. I gave her and Fred hell. I said, "You know what Dr. Stern said." Lina said she was being monitored by a doctor each month.

Tony, Jr. was discharged from the army and working on one of the farms in New York State. Mike told me when we needed more help that Tony, Jr., would like to work with us. I told Mike to tell Tony to give notice to whom he was working for and let me know when he could come to work. He would have to get a room somewhere between us. I went out looking for more work. About a month later Tony, Jr., was working with us. With myself, I had a seven-man crew now.

Lina was due to have a baby any day now. Bette was pregnant with our second child, and Mike's wife, Marie, was pregnant, too.

We got a call from Fred. Lina died getting ready to go to the hospital. She fainted on the kitchen floor of their

apartment. Fred got in his car (they lived five minutes from the doctor's office), raced there, and got the doctor, and they raced back to the apartment. Lina was dead!! As a matter of fact, Lina was dead when she hit the floor. The doctor asked Fred for a knife. Fred gave him a kitchen knife, He cut Lina's belly open to try to save the baby. It was too long a time. The baby, a pretty little girl, fully developed, with a full head of black hair, suffocated. Fred went to pieces. At the autopsy they found that Lina's heart was one big ball of scar tissue. With the excitement of going to the hospital, her heart split in half. There was no room for expansion as her blood pressure rose, it just split her heart in half. Lina was twenty-eight years old.

We were back in the rat race only a couple of months. My Uncle Clarence called Bette to tell us that Grandpa had died and my mother was being uncivil to everyone. Bette didn't know where I was working. I had seven or eight jobs going at one time, and they were all in different stages of completion. When I got home I told Bette to take it easy; I'd call Clarence after supper. Bette was pregnant and sick, preoccupied all day. I said, "First of all, I don't believe with all my aunts and uncles that are there, you mean to tell me one of them won't look after their sister?" Bette said, "It looks like we are elected to take Frances." We had a year-and-a-half-old baby daughter and Bette was about six months pregnant, and we lived on the third floor. Bette was really down. I said, "I'll see. Maybe one of the aunts might want her."

When Mike, Tony, Jr., and I arrived at Grandpa's house, the aunts and uncles were arguing about Maggie being in the house and staying in the house. Eugene was saying to me, pointing his finger at me, "It's all your fault. You should have taken care of Maggie." I reminded him, "When Tony died, Grandpa said he was taking Maggie

home with him. I said then she should be in a hospital. No one said a word then. Bette and I came up to visit Grandpa and Maggie every month or so. Grandpa never said anything. How many times did you see your father in the last year? Last fall I came up to visit Grandpa; he was reroofing the house. I carried enough shingles on to the roof so he could shingle the back side. I asked why he didn't call any of you to help him. Grandpa said he wanted quality help. I said, 'I'll come up next weekend and help you finish the roof.' He said, no, he wanted something to do; he only worked for about four hours a day. About three weeks from then he would be ready for the other half of the shingles to be taken up. I came up and put the shingles on the roof for him. Nothing was ever said that he was having trouble with Maggie. We knew Maggie wasn't doing anything. When we came, there was nothing to snack on. I offered to get something. They did not want anything. They said they had just finished eating."

Eugene asked, "What are you going to do with Maggie?"

"Put her in a hospital," I said.

"Where is she going to stay until then?"

I said, "Right here."

My aunts called the family doctor, he arranged an examination with two other doctors. During the examination, as the doctors were talking and examining Maggie, Mike started to cry. The doctors signed papers recommending that Maggie be committed to a mental hospital. Maggie was put in a hospital after we buried Grandpa. Bette and I took France and went home to New Jersey.

When we got home and told the landlord what had happened and we were looking for a bigger apartment,

he understood! Bette had her second baby on the twentieth of September 1956. The first of October we moved to a new apartment on the first floor of a two-family in Maplewood, about four blocks from Bette's mother's apartment.

Bette was under a great strain, with two babies and a five-year-old sister-in-law who had been allowed to grow up wild. Frances still ate with her hands and did not know how to hold a fork or spoon to eat with. She didn't care to learn, did many things for spite, and was very jealous of the two babies. All the instruction and scolding just made matters worse. Frances was not talking; I couldn't even get her to shake her head yes or no. It got really bad. Bette and I would be at each other.

Mike was getting sick again; he started to fail. Marie had her baby a few months after Bette had Hank, Jr.

We started to try to see if we could get Frances to open up with therapy. After a few sessions the therapist told us if we worked around her we would get along. We needed some nitwit to tell us if we let Frances shit on us and we would get along. Somewhere, somehow, this therapist got the situation confused. That was why we were here, to get help because Frances was shitting on us. That ended that kind of approach.

The next thing was through the church. There was a Catholic school for girls in Kearney, about an hour away. It took a month or so, but we finally got Frances in the school. I would go and get her on weekends. After work on Friday I would go and pick up Frances at the school and late on Sunday afternoon I would bring her back to school. This made more work for Bette and a lot more work for me, too. It gave Bette a little relief during the day, but the guilt Bette had for not being able to keep Frances home all the time was weighing heavily on her.

Bette was not happy at all that Frances was at Saint Anthony's School. When Frances came home every second weekend and holidays. Bette would have mixed emotions about sending Frances back to school again. It just tortured her so. I think what made it even worse for was the fact that it did not bother me if Frances was with us or the school. I learned a long time ago you will survive. The sad part of it, in the early days that Frances was at the school, was that I don't think it bothered Frances, either. Bette was the one sick over it.

At that time I was doing a big industrial building; I had labor problems and a lot on my mind. I thought I would have union troubles, so I went to the union hall to speak to the delegate. He had no men to give me. I asked him, "Where am I going to get six men for about three months?"

He said, "I can't help you. You will have to get your own men."

I put an ad in the paper: "Help wanted, laborers." I got a good response. I hired eight more men, all unskilled. That never bothered me; if they were willing to work I would teach them. I taught most of the men I hired to do things my way anyway.

We were working about two weeks and the labor delegate I went to see dropped in and told me he wanted to unionize my men. I just kept on working and ignored him. Everything he said, I said yes to. I don't know what he said; I was not listening to what he said. The next week he came back while we were on a coffee break. He said to me, "You did not come to my office to sign up your men for dues."

I said, "You got to be kidding."

He went over to the men and said something to them. All the new men picked up their tools and left. Then he

said to me, "I have some paperwork in my trunk for you." He opened the trunk; the only thing lying in the trunk was a .45-caliber pistol. This man was over six feet eight inches, with a fifty-inch waist and weighed 300 pounds, a big slob. I turned to him and looked him right in the eye. I stuck my finger in his belly button, which was as high off the ground as the nipples on my breasts. The saliva in my mouth dried right up. I could not speak for a tenth of a second, and when I opened my mouth my voice was ten octaves higher. I sounded like Tiny Tim tiptoeing through the tulips. My voice was squeaky and tinny. It was so high-pitched I could not believe I sounded like such a wimp. But, I'll tell you, our eyes locked onto each other for about thirty seconds. I don't know what kind of look I gave him, but his face showed to me surprise, then fear. I was so mad at that point. He slammed the trunk closed, hurried to his car, and said, "You be at my office in the morning." I didn't tell my brothers or anyone what had happened. There were five of us, all told, now to do the job.

The next morning I put my twelve-gauge double-barreled shotgun in the back of the seat in my 1947 Dodge truck, four double-aught buckshot in the glove compartment, one double-aught buck in my right front pocket, and one double-aught buck in my left front pocket. The job was about thirty miles from home. I waited for my two brothers to come, and when they did we went to work. I never went to the delegate's offices, never! I kept on working; after a few days the double-aught buck started to leave a worn impression in my trousers. Mike said to me at coffee break, "What are you carrying the coins in your pocket for? Forget to take them out last night?" I paid the men in cash and on Thursday nights I would go to the bank and get the money needed to make payroll.

Bette asked me, too, what I was carrying around in my pockets. I told her the marks were from rolls of coins from the bank. I told my brothers and the two men working for me about a month later. I never told Bette until thirty years later. We finished the building and the delegate never came around anymore, either.

Mike's Hodgkin's disease crippled him again that winter. He never knew that he had Hodgkin's, to our knowledge. The doctor started Mike on radiation treatments again, every couple of weeks.

I was earning a little more money now. The first couple of years after paying all the bills and buying tools and other equipment that was needed for work, there was never any money left.

Bette and I started to look around for land that I could build a house on for us. I thought I was smart at twenty-eight years old. We went to Morris County, one of the richest counties in Northern New Jersey; then I started to look for the town with the cheapest real estate tax. I found Randolph Township was really rural, with one cop; everything and every office in the town hall was part-time. We bought seven acres on a dirt road. There were only two houses on Everdale Road in 1956. I didn't have enough money to pay for the land outright. I was able to put $1,000 down and pay whatever I could pay a month. I paid the $4,000 off in a year. Then I would go to the lot on weekends and cut trees to clear the land for the house. I drew the plans for my house and over the next couple of years, while trying to save money to build, Bette and I changed the floor plan many times.

Mike's health got so bad he could not work anymore. As a matter of fact, he could not walk very much. He could move around his apartment and watch his baby while his wife, Marie, worked. Her insurance covered

most of his medical bills. There was a drug that helped him. The insurance covered only one prescription a month. Mike would use it up in a couple of weeks. I used to stop and see him once a week on the way home from work. I would give him some money, and I would go see the pharmacist and talk the pharmacist into giving me the drug without the prescription for Mike.

Tony, Jr., was starting to behave like he did when he was a kid back in 1940 on the farm. He did not come in to work for a couple of days in the week. I asked him what the problem was. He didn't think he should have to help give Mike some money. Then he said, "The other day when he last saw Mike he had his shotgun standing in the corner of the living room."

I said, "So?"

Tony, Jr., told me I should go over to Mike's and take the gun away from him.

I said, "You were there; why didn't you take it?"

Tony said, "You know how Mike is. I don't think he would give it to me."

I said, "What makes you think he would give it to me?"

I went over to see Mike. When he answered the door, before I said hello or he let me in, Mike said, "The shotgun stays."

I said, "All right." I gave him some money and the prescription of drugs he used.

Mike said, "Don't buy any more drugs. They're not working anymore."

I said, "What the hell is the matter with Tony?"

Mike said, "I really don't know. Tony wanted to leave months ago."

I said to Mike, "He can go anytime he wants to."

Mike said, "Tony doesn't like the idea that you keep asking him to spend a weekend with his sister Frances."

I said, "Tony goes upstate every weekend. He doesn't come to work on Monday anymore, he shows up on Tuesday, and he doesn't come in on Friday. He doesn't tell me what he is doing. Tony doesn't talk at all anymore. He has a scowl on his face all the time."

Mike said, "He wants you to fire him."

I guess he never did grow up; he was back to his old habits as a kid.

A few days after I saw Mike, Tony asked me one morning if I went to see Mike. I said, no, I was too busy. Tony didn't say any more. He did not come to work for a couple of days. I thought he had quit. I started a new job with the other two men I had working for me, so I didn't see Tony for another week. Tony was hanging out in the coffee shop that I usually went to get coffee for our coffee break. He wanted his couple of days' pay. I said, "You will have to come back tomorrow." Tony came back the next day for his pay. I gave him the money. He didn't even look at me; he approached me cowardly. He was looking down at the ground. I don't know how he saw my hand with his pay envelope in it. Tony grabbed it and turned around and left. We did not exchange words. Later that week when I went to see Mike, Mike told me Tony and a kid he had gone to school with named Herb had gone into farming together.

"Why didn't you tell me?" I said to Mike.

"I wanted him to tell you."

"I don't see that partnership lasting very long," I said.

Mike's Hodgkin's disease got worse. He had to be put in the hospital, St. Michael's in Newark. Mike died in the spring of 1959 at twenty-eight years of age.

I had four men working for me at that time. I worked, too.

Bette was anxious for us to start our house. For me to save enough money to build the house would take too long. So the next rainy day I went to a couple of banks, plus the one I did business with, and filled out loan applications. I took the plans that I drew up to the building inspector to look over. Bette could not wait for a rainy day for me to go to see the inspector again. I had to work with my men; I was the only skilled one on the job. I had to work or I made no money. Bette took a train to Randolph to the building inspector's office. She got all the permits required to start construction. I started to build my house before I got the loan. I would work for a paying customer, then work on my house for a few days, then for a customer for a week or two, then back to my house. I did this in 1959 and 1960. I got my loan in the spring of 1960. I wanted $66,000 to build my house; that was to be 90 percent of the cost. They gave me 50 percent, $34,000. I spent all of that plus money I earned, and I paid my men when I had them work on my house. I figured my house cost me around $75,000 to build in 1960. We moved in July of 1961. The kitchen, bathroom, and bedroom were done. My living room was not finished. It was, or is, twenty-eight feet wide by thirty-four feet long with a fifteen-foot ceiling height. I had a scaffold in my living room for more than nine months, as I was working on the ceiling. I did not work on the ceiling steady! The living room was finished in cherry wood and looks beautiful.

In the spring of 1961 Tony came to my new house with his girlfriend. He wanted to know if I would hire him! I said, "What happened to farming?"

Tony said, "We can't make enough money for two families to live on."

I told him, "Right now I don't have an opening. I'm not going to lay a man off to hire you, not the way you left me. I have a few things I'm going to ask you to think about if you decide to come back to work for me. Once a month you will pick Frances, your sister, up from school and spend some time with her. And every three months or so I want you to go and see your mother in the hospital. You haven't seen any of your family since you left two years ago. I happen to know you and Herb went your separate ways months ago." On my way back from seeing Maggie I would stop in New Paltz to visit Lina's grave; then I would stop to see our father's grave. Then the next time I would go to Mike's grave; it was too far to visit all three graves in one trip. I would see someone on those trips who kept me informed. Tony agreed and came to work for me the second time in late summer of 1961. Later that year Tony married.

I had the house behind me now. There were a lot of things that had to be done, like sidewalks, lawn, and driveway. I was able to do them at night after my regular work and weekends. I worked harder now than I ever had worked.

I was so busy that I lost count of the promise Tony had made to me about going to see Maggie and his sister Frances! In those two years he saw Maggie twice and his sister Frances three times. The third time Tony went to the school for Frances he brought her to our house and dumped her off with Bette. That Saturday, as usual, I was out giving estimates, talking to customers, collecting money and lining up work for the following week. When I came home we had planned to go to the beach that Sunday. Frances had to be back at school by 6:00 P.M. on

Sunday. Tony was not answering his phone. We did not go anywhere.

Tony was starting to act contemptuous again. This spring he was starting the silent and grunting routine again. Tony had a problem; sometimes I thought he hated me. He would not help me in any way, he would not give me any of his time, he would not say thank you when I did him a favor, and I did many. He acted like a stranger and treated me as if I were a stranger. I don't know why he stayed working for me. His young life was really tough on him; being dumped in that crude lifestyle at six years old was quite a shock. That is the way it was. Everyone else rolled with the punches, so to speak. But not Tony. We grow older and wiser (I thought). That Monday morning at work I asked him what the stunt was supposed to be about. Tony said he forgot about Frances. I said, "Tony, I've had it with you. I don't know why you hate me so. You actually cringe when I come near you. Your body actions show fear and discomfort. If you are that unhappy why do you stay?!? If you don't say what is on your mind it will never be resolved. Tony, I'm giving you notice. It's the end of June now, I want you gone by Labor Day, if not sooner. I'm not putting up with this shit anymore. You're my brother and married; you've got two months to find another job. You can go anytime between now and Labor Day. When you don't come in to work anymore, I'll know you have quit."

Tony said, "You are not my brother and Frances is not my sister."

I said, "Have it your way, Tony."

We worked that summer, Tony not talking to me. I gave him instructions in the morning. Tony stayed until Labor Day. I paid him his money; he didn't say a word. He would not look at me, just got in his car and left,

September 1962. I don't know what he told people. On occasion someone would say to me, "You don't talk to your brother. Some of these people, I didn't know who they were. I never said anything. I don't know what the trouble was with Tony. Just last month (June, 2000) someone said to me, "You still don't talk to your brother." I just looked at him with a questioning stare. I didn't say a word; he got nervous and moved on. Tony has been gone thirty-seven years.

There was a lot of building going on in New Jersey at that time. I had people waiting three to four months for me to do their work. So I decided to hire more men. For about two years I had twenty-two men working for me. I built a bowling alley, four factories, a number of shops, and a couple of houses. The winter of 1963–64 was a very cold one. Right after Thanksgiving we started having a snowstorm a week, four to eight inches each time. The temperature went down at night from zero degrees to ten below zero. It never went over twenty-five degrees for the high until February. The frost was four feet deep; water and sanitary sewer lines froze and broke everywhere. We finished doing all the inside work and could not work outside. By the end of January I laid everyone off.

March of 1964 I was at my bookkeeper's office; we were going over receipts, expenses, insurance, and taxes. I found out that I had two more partners. The insurance company and the federal government each took a third of the money I brought in, and I was working twelve to fourteen hours a day, even on Sundays. The money that I put in my pocket was only a couple of thousand dollars more than when I had four men and myself working. I said I was a fast learner. When I started up again in April 1964, I hired three more men who were on a steady

payroll. If I needed more men for a week or two, I would go to the union hall for help.

In a few months it would be winter and I wanted to take some time off and go hunting. So, I did not hire anyone and stalled new work until spring. Near the end of October, Peter Anthony, a tailor of men's clothes, wanted to build a new building on a main street in Maplewood, New Jersey. I told him I was not interested. The job would have to be 100 percent union. The delegate in this area was a rotten son of a bitch! Peter said he talked to him. The delegate said I could keep my men and we had to take three men from his union and one of his men was to be shop steward. He got paid twenty-five cents more per hour. Peter had a meeting in his old tailor shop, the delegate from the labor union and myself. Peter gave him a couple of fine suits and I don't know how much cash. The delegate said anytime we needed more men they would come from their union. Everybody shook hands, done deal. After he left I said to Peter, "I don't trust him. That kind are rotten people. I have had to deal with them at different times, and their word does not mean anything to them. I've been threatened they're going to stop the job. If I give them a dollar they will want more." Never give them a nickel; they would go to the owner and harass him. Some gave in and some did not.

By the time we got an excavator on the job, it was around the twentieth of November. I could not believe the weather, no snow, no cold air, the temperature was sixty-five degrees during the day. Three days into the digging of the cellar, we were finishing the hole, around 2:00 P.M. on the twenty-second of November, and someone was hollering, running up the street. The president has been shot! I was ten feet below the sidewalk in a big hole in the ground, seventy-five by 100 feet on Springfield

Avenue in Maplewood. They say everybody remembers where and what they were doing on that day that Kennedy was killed. That's where I was. I'm going to tell you another reason that I remember that spot of ground, which makes it two lasting memories.

The union delegate sent only one man. It didn't matter; I had my three men. This laborer from the union hall was just a gofer. By the end of the day we found out he was picked up off the street and was told he had to go to work and to report on the job every day. The rest of the week we installed forms for the footing of the building. We had sixty yards of concrete ordered for Monday morning to pour the footing. I lived forty-five minutes away. I left the house a little earlier than usual. As I pulled up to the job there was a crowd of people at the job site. I thought someone fell through our barricade into the hole. No such luck! It was a picket line of about fifty men. I got to a phone really quick and called the concrete company. I told them what was going on. I told them the whole deal. The man from the union hall, who had three days' pay coming, was in the picket line. I said, "I'll call you later when I find out something."

The dispatcher asked if my forms were done and still in good shape to pour.

I said, "Yes."

This company had union drivers, and half the drivers hated this man. They said they would deliver if I would take the concrete. I said, "OK." The delegate showed up with two armed thugs. I said to him, "All right, what the hell is the story now?"

One of the thugs was his twenty-eight-year-old son, and he said to me, "You talk to my father with respect."

I turned to him and said, "Fuck you."

He came over to me and pushed his body against me, shoving the handle of the pistol under his jacket in my face. This was now the ninth or tenth time in the few years that I had been in business that this stunt was pulled on me.

His father told him to stop. Then the father said to me, in broken English, with a heavy Italian accent, "You have to sign on as one of my contractors and I have to use union help wherever I work."

I said, "You're nuts! Ninety percent of my work is private homes."

The delegate said to me, "Then you stay there."

I said to him, "You are right! The only reason I'm here is because Peter paid you off. You made a deal with us! For some reason, Peter thinks I'm the only one that can build his building."

At that point the first concrete truck pulled up. The men on the picket line crawled all over the truck, like ants, and the language they used on the poor driver, I never heard some of the phrases. The driver was about sixty. I thought he was going to have a heart attack! I said to the driver, "Forget it. Take the truck back."

He said, "No. I was given orders to unload. If I come back with concrete in my truck I will be fired."

I said, "Let's go, then."

We poured the footing with all these men hollering obscenities at us. When the last truck was done most of the men were gone. One of the men who was in the picket line came to me. He said, "Why don't you sign up?"

I said, "We made a deal. That was not on the table at the time we talked."

The laborer said, "We have no men to give you. None of our men are out of work. As a matter of fact, he needs men and he wants your three men."

I said, "That figures."

"We have to come and picket or we don't work."

I said, "I know it. From the fifty men the first day it is down to fifteen today. We are taking the forms off the footing and waiting for block to be delivered."

The first load of concrete block arrived early in the morning. We had a hard time with the picket line not letting the driver in to unload. I was to have sand and cement delivered, too. No more material came. At lunch time I went to the supply yard and asked, "What happened to my stuff?"

Mr. Salmon said, "Hank, you are a good customer of ours. The delegate came here and threatened all kinds of things. Hank, I can't send you any more material. Don't even pay me for the load of block I sent over."

I called four or five more places. I told them up front what happened. They all sent the material, but the drivers would not come onto the job site to unload. The pickets, shouts, and profanity drove the drivers away. None of the supply houses that I had been buying from would send me any material. I said to Peter, "No one will send us anything. I told you he was a rotten son of a bitch!"

Peter said, "What am I going to do?"

"I told you to hire a union contractor." Peter said, "There was no one available. Besides, I want you to build my building."

I said, "I could have been a consultant."

Peter said, "Find me a contractor."

I said, "Let me think about it. I'll get back to you."

That weekend I was out making my rounds, taking care of complaints and collecting money. On my way home I stopped to see a young man who was trying to start a mason supply yard. I asked him if he would be

interested in supplying the concrete block for the basement of this building. I told him the whole story, about the union and the picket line. Arty said, "What else is the building being built with?"

I told him, "It's only a one-story, about sixteen feet high above the sidewalk, out of block and brick, wood timbers for rafters, sheet rock, and the usual stuff inside."

Arty said, "If you order everything through me, I'll bring it into the job site."

I said, "Give me a few days."

Monday I spoke with Peter. I told him, "I have a man that will cross the picket line."

Peter says, "Are you sure?"

"Yes, he is just starting this supply company. You will have to pay him every week. He doesn't have much of a credit line."

Peter asked, "What makes you think he will deliver?"

"He is hungry. Hungry men will do anything. I know; I was there!"

"What happened to you?" Peter said. "I thought you finally got what you wanted just to be a consultant."

I said, "I don't know who the contractor would be and he might give me more of a headache than this delegate. I have nothing to do for this winter. I'm winning with this guy. Now that I found this guy, Arty, I'll shove this job up that delegate's ass. You ready for some rough stuff? This guy won't go away quietly."

Peter said, "OK."

I got hold of Arty and he came with the first load of block. The men in the picket line started to climb onto his truck. Arty said to the men, "If you value your life, get our ass off my truck," and drove right in onto the job site. The men had to run or he would have run over them.

I was there with my three men, moving the block into the hole for the foundation. The second day Arty brought more block; the picket lines parted and let the truck in to the job. Around coffee break time (9:30 A.M.) there were a dozen or so men in the picket line and the two thugs showed ups. They were talking to their men in the picket line with their jackets open, braszenly showing off their pistols in their shoulder holsters. I said I was a fast learner. I went to my pickup and from the back of the seat I took out two guns wrapped in my navy blanket. One was a semiautomatic twelve-gauge shotgun; the other was a bolt-action 30-06 Springfield military rifle, 1903 vintage, this rifle I hunted in NY State for deer. I laid them on the tailgate of my truck. I put the guns in the back of my seat of the truck two weeks earlier. I was waiting for this time, to call this bully's bluff. Well! Half the men in the picket line left. I was showing my men the guns, explaining how they worked, the semiautomatic when opened to chamber a shell and closed when empty made a very big noise. I did this several times. We stayed by my truck passing the guns back and forth to one another until the punks left.

We worked whenever the weather was warm enough to work. I showed up on the job every day, and every day there were four to six men picketing, walking up and down the street until noon. It took all winter to build the foundation. The weather was more of a problem than the union. The men walked the picket line for almost six months. When the roofer pulled onto the job to install the hot roof, the picketing stopped, and those two thugs with the pistols never came back after my display of my arms.

Arty became my main supplier for materials. He grew bigger, has quite a nice yard now, and is doing great.

I worked over the years with three to eight men, all according to the amount of work I had to do.

I never went to the union delegates anymore. In those first few years I thought that was the way to handle the situation. I found out it was better to go on as if they did not exist, and when they came around to shut the job down I laughed at them and would tell a fib of a story: "I wished you would. I did not want to be here, so if you stop the job for me, I'll be able to go to another job where I can make some money. This job is a dead one. I owe this guy a favor. He helped me out a few years ago, now he wants this job done, and I need to get away for at least a month." I would keep on working and say, "Bring on the pickets in the morning," and I would laugh. "We will have coffee together in the morning."

I never had any more trouble with the unions other than a delegate trying to get some cash. I never paid any of them. I carried my old double-barrel shotgun in my truck for years, waiting for the next time I was shown a gun by a delegate. I planned on going to my truck to show him what I had. It never happened. There was a lot of talk but no more muscle.

Bette's life was the children and her house and furniture. Bette, like myself, came from a very poor family. My father-in-law borrowed fifty dollars to give us something at our wedding. My father, Tony, didn't give us a nickel, and he didn't come to our wedding, either, saying he could not get anyone to milk the cows. The money Bette and I got at our wedding just paid for the wedding. We lived in suburbia. Bette had to drive the kids everywhere, doctors, dentists, baseball, ballet, food, shopping, whatever!

I was busy with my work. We never went on a full week's vacation. I was very busy in the summertime and

never knew what the winter would bring. We would go on long weekend trips, leaving Friday night and coming back on Monday.

Frances turned sixteen and the school did not keep the girls over sixteen. Rather than have the school place her in a foster home, Bette and I had decided to try and finish raising Frances. It worked out well. Frances and Bette became friends and got along quite well together.

Most of the men who worked for me only worked a couple of years. They would find other work because the work with me was not steady. Almost every winter we could not work outside doing mason work. These men moved on to a more secure type work. I started to think of what would I do for a retirement plan when I got older. I thought about stocks . . . what stocks? I knew nothing about investing money. I started to read the business section of the paper. I was inquiring about different stocks, checking this and that. It seemed impossible to pick something that I felt comfortable with. Then one day in the paper there was an offer to buy stock for a new bank just being formed. As a kid I remembered that the men I worked with and around would always say, "You make money with money," or "you have to have money to make money." So a little lightbulb lit up: invest in a bank. So I did. I called the number and I was referred to the National Union Bank to pick up the forms. The National Union Bank was the bank I had been working with the past eight years. I had a checking and a little savings account, and over the years I borrowed money when I was short for a payroll and paid it back on time. I had a good credit line.

When I went to get the forms a Mr. Green said to me, "Do you have any National Union stock?"

I said, "No."

He said, "I'll give you the forms, but it would help if you had some of our bank stock."

I said, "How do I get some?"

Mr. Green said, "It's not for sale on the market. We are a private bank."

A month later I'm in the bank for payroll money. I went every week for payroll. Mr. Green said, "Hank, I don't have your form or money for the new issue of stock."

I said, "What in the hell should I file for? You said unless I had some stock in this bank I wouldn't even be considered."

Mr. Green said an old stock holder in the bank had just died and the children were selling her stock in the bank. "How much do you want?"

I said, "How much do I need to qualify?"

"One hundred shares should do it."

I said, "Put me down for one hundred shares."

When I brought the other forms in the next week Mr. Green said, "Ask for double of what you want. We are having such a good response to the issue they are going to accept fifty percent of what is being asked for!"

Guess what? I was given what I asked for; now I was strapped for ready cash. I had to tighten my belt that year. Every year there was a new bank being formed and I would buy a few hundred shares all through the seventies and eighties. A few years would go by and the bank stock would have a stock split, two for one or a four for 1, whatever, and then they started to pay dividends, which I reinvested back into the bank. Then in the late eighties and early nineties the banks started to buy each other. At one time I must have had stock in a dozen banks or so. Now I had stock in two banks and I never sold a share. With the mergers and buyouts and stock splits over the years, I did very well. When I turned sixty-two

years of age I was able to retire. When I was around forty-five I thought I would have to work until I died. Things really came together for me. I said earlier that my childhood was tough; my adult life was not easy, either. I worked hard and I had to literally fight to work and be myself. I wanted to be independent. If I had to live my life over, it would not bother me if it went the same way; every day it got better. I was always happy. I looked forward to the next day and the challenge it brought forward. Crazy, hugh! I was a happy man and still am. I only wish Mike and Lina lived a little longer.

I retired at sixty-two years of age, and people still hound me to do work for them. In order to stop I had to sell my truck and give away or sell most of my equipment.

I played golf for a few years until I broke 100 and went fishing now and then. I go on longer hunting trips now and more of them and help my friends and neighbors do little projects.

Bette and I planned to do a little traveling. Bette's allergies as she got into her sixties started to get worse. She had allergies all her life. She took her allergy medicine and shots in her arms weekly for years to control the allergies. Now everything turned against her. The medicine started to be a problem. Bette got very ill and could not eat anything without a reaction. After many tests, seeing many doctors, Bette can't take any medicine of any kind. She is allergic to all of them and limited as to foods that she can eat. Bette is now developing cataracts. She can't have the operation because she can't use the medicine needed for recuperation. Bette maintained her weight all her life; she would go from 109 to 112 pounds always. Now Bette was losing about one and one-half pounds a month; she could not gain any weight. We went to many doctors to find out the problem. Every one

of these specialists thought he could solve the problem. After Bette went five or six months, they told her that she could not help her anymore. We would go to another specialist and another specialist. We went to New York City, Connecticut, Pennsylvania, and four more in New Jersey. In the meantime Bette was losing weight; she was down to eighty-eight pounds now. We started to see this specialist in September of 1999. He stopped Bette from losing any more weight. We go to see him twice a week; he has Bette eating a few more foods than she had in the past. She had gained a few pounds since we started to see him. In the middle of May 2000, Bette did not respond to the treatment anymore and lapsed back to her old reactions to the food.

The doctor, Dr. Scott P. Huber, was disappointed, but he said, "We will have to start over again; somewhere we missed something." This is the first doctor who did not say, "I can't do any more for you." Bette is allergic to herself. Just about everything she eats Bette has a bad reaction of some kind to.

Bette is a self-taught accomplished artist (watercolors). She has taken a best in show, a runner-up, and three honorable mentions in the few years that she has been painting. Now the cataracts are hindering her in just about everything she does. Bette has been a Yankee fan all her life; she knows all the players. I don't. She followed football. Bette is active in politics, and writes and calls Washington, D.C., Trenton, New Jersey, and our local government. Bette is a spunky, gutsy, fighting little lady. She has a miniature medical library that she refers to now and then to help herself. Bette will talk to the doctors on their terms and using their language. The girl is smart.

This story is mainly about me, to explain to my children how I had an ambition to succeed in my pursuit to be rich and independent, that I wished I spent more quality time with them, more than I did. I got caught up in the rat race, and I enjoyed it. I never did discuss my work with my family. It would be dull; plus some of the personalities I dealt with would be sheer horror and the misunderstandings and the lying that went on I wanted to forget about, not be reminded of the troubles I had all day. I know you don't go anywhere beating a dead horse!

Bette and I have two grown children, a daughter married over twenty years with two children (boys), and a son, married only a few years, no children yet. My sister, Frances, has been married close to thirty years, and has two children (boys).

In my retirement I take Bette to the doctors at least twice a week, sometimes three. I belong to a beagle club. We have fifty-seven acres in Sussex County. Across the road from the beagle club my son and I have a wood lot. When I get the chance I go to do some field work on the grounds.

How I got to write these stories was just an accident. I will explain.

Early in 1997 I received a phone call from a pleasant-speaking lady from the Naval Special Warfare Archives (http://www.navyfrogmen.com) inquiring about UDT. This nice lady's name was Pamela J. Russell. She and her husband, R. D. Russell, formed the archives to log in information about UDT and the SEALs. There are a lot of blank months and names missing in the telling of UDT. At the time I went through training there were no logs or ledgers or records of any kind kept.

Pam had seen an article I had sent to the *Blast,* a quarterly magazine about the navy, UDT and the SEALs.

Now and then I would comment on an article or send a picture or two and sometimes a funny story that happened when I was in UDT. In our correspondence I elected to write a story of what I remembered about my hitch in UDT to help Pam understand what went on at Little Creek in UDT.

After writing "1945–50, My Navy Years," I thought my childhood years should be told. Now I'm finishing 1950–2000. It is to let my family know what I went through to provide a good life for them and their future.

All stories have an ending.

Epilogue

After I was discharged from the Navy, I could not get a steady job near my hometown area. The only company hiring was IBM, and they had a two-year waiting list. Everyone I went to see that advertised for help was reluctant to hire me. Some of the responses were as follows: One foreman of a company said to me, "If I hire you, in a couple of months you will have my job." Another said, "You won't stay here long. As soon as you get a better offer you will be gone." Another one said, "I want someone that is desperate. If I hire you, in about a year you will take over my business." Because of these people's apprehensiveness to deal with me, that is the big reason I took Uncle Nick's offer to come to New Jersey.

I don't know if I would have lasted as a diesel mechanic. I really did not like grease and oil to play in.

My Aunt Terry still believed until she died that I knew that they served cat and rat at Captain Joe's.

My going to Arthur Murray's, where I met Bette, was one of my better decisions. If Bette was not homesick and the humid air in Florida was not terrible, we could easily have stayed in Florida.

My Uncle Nick did me a favor when he fired me. That was the first and only time I was ever fired.

Harry and Jimmy were a big help to me in getting started into business for myself. I learned a lot about people when dealing with them when I was in business. I became pretty good at sizing up a situation.

Most of the men who worked for me were going to college. Some worked for me four seasons, some two. They were very strong men. They were football players or into another sport in college.

It's a shame that my brother Tony couldn't get over his offensive attitude toward me.

Over the years Bette was a good mother to her children and a great wife to me. We were so busy with our responsibilities in those early years of raising the kids and getting all the material things we wanted that since I retired we really are getting to know each other.

Last but not least, I have to thank Pam Russell for inquiring about UDT Four of me a few years ago or I might not have written this story.

As I was getting ready to send this last part of my story to Pam to make a booklet for me, in the newspaper this past week of October 6, year 2000, the nation's eighth-largest bank is buying New Jersey's largest bank, which is great for me. I have a few shares of New Jersey's largest bank.

Every day it gets better.